Style and Communication in the English Language

Randolph Quirk

Vice-Chancellor, University of London

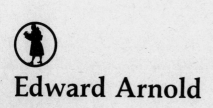

Edward Arnold

© Randolph Quirk 1982

First published 1982 by
Edward Arnold (Publishers) Ltd
41 Bedford Square, London WC1B 3DQ

British Library Cataloguing in Publication Data

Quirk, Randolph
    Style and communication in the English language.
    1. English language—Style
    I. Title
    808   PE1421

ISBN 0-7131-6260-0

Text set in 10/12pt Paladium Medium Compugraphic by
Colset (Private) Ltd.
Printed and bound by Richard Clay (The Chaucer Press) Ltd,
Bungay, Suffolk

Contents

Foreword

Like many other writers on specialized topics in linguistics, I have always been interested in broader topics too. Like other linguists again, I have therefore felt the urge to write from time to time on such sweeping themes as 'style' and even 'communication'. Never a book, of course. Who could have the brash confidence, the sheer effrontery, to write a book on style and communication, still less a book called *Style and Communication*?

And yet as I have chanced my arm in recent years on individual aspects of these global areas, it has been represented to me that through these separate products of quite disparate stimuli there ran a theme: that the effectiveness and even the meaning itself of a communication were indissociable from the style in which it was couched. In other words, it is dangerously superficial to regard 'style' as giving to 'communication' a mere top-dressing: pleasant enough if you have the skill or the time to lay it on but essentially inessential and understandably dispensable in hard times.

This is brought sharply home to practitioners in certain professions. Flight-deck crews are severely constrained to make their radio communications according to strict stylistic rules which lay down both the form and the order for presenting data like identity, position, time, altitude, etc:

London Control GBFBO Daventry at 47
flight level 80 estimating Lichfield at 0901

Even a style of pronunciation is prescribed: *five* must be 'fife' and *three* 'tree'. Style and communication are inseparable.

A Member of Parliament is forbidden to say that another Member is a liar, but he may communicate his conviction of this if he couches it in the appropriate parliamentary style. And of course, now we are thinking about it, far more humdrum examples spring to mind. A recent article in the London *Sunday Times* commented on the studiously alert language of doormen in exclusive clubs. The stranger who is met with the inquiry 'Can I help you, sir?' is in fact being firmly challenged to demonstrate his right of access.

The interaction and inseparability of style and communication are examined in this book with respect to some of the more obviously interesting areas. There is broadcasting, for example. There are the emotion-charged symbols of nationhood, ancient or emergent. There is the rapid adjustment in recent years to sexual permissiveness on the one hand and to racial susceptibilities on the other.

But knowing, as Robert Frost says, 'how way leads on to way', no-one should be surprised that some of the paths I tread are more unexpected. I devote a good deal of space to dictionaries and the way their style and content both reflect and (to a lesser extent) determine current communication concerns. I examine the relation of style and grammar to a class of nouns whose meaning has been affected by the impact of 'folk statistics' and mass communication. And I end by exploring the way in which the form of that most archetypally 'literary' genre, the lyric, reflects communication strategies that are inherent in the most prosaic forms of everyday dialogue.

All of the chapters have appeared elsewhere but none has been reprinted in its original form. In the necessary work of revision and adaptation, I have been fortunate to enjoy skilled advice from the publishers, to whose credit indeed lies the very idea of producing this volume.

Randolph Quirk

Senate House,
London WC1
July 1982

1 Speaking into the Air

When Edmund Burke seized upon the idea of the press as the fourth estate (implying equal power with the commons, the lords, and the church), he was helping to elevate the media to a position far above their station.[1] When *The Times Educational Supplement* in 1932 called radio the fifth estate, a still greater flattery was perpetrated and the BBC has needed little encouragement to try and live up to it. In this spirit, Andrew Timothy, following a month's scrutiny of radio output, concludes that 'the BBC has a clear duty to uphold the standards of spoken English', a plea that seeks support from an unattributed quotation in the form of a resounding rhetorical question: 'For if the trumpet give an uncertain sound, who shall prepare himself to the battle?' (Burchfield *et al.* 1979, 24). But Mr Timothy might well have gone on and given the next verse from this Pauline epistle (1 Corinthians 9): 'except you utter . . . plain speech, how shall it be known what is said? For you will be speaking into the air.'

Self-evidently, it is the BBC's first responsibility to ensure that it 'be known what is said', and it is only to this end (and not, for instance, for the sake of language standards *per se*) that the duty to 'uphold the standards of spoken English' arises. When one reflects on the range of listeners and viewers that are to be addressed, themselves observing a range of language standards of which pitifully little is known, the perceived 'duty' becomes as bewildering as it does onerous. When one further reflects on the amount of broadcasting throughout which the duty is to be maintained (in 1979, over 420 hours a day in the UK services alone), it may well seem that the

Note: This chapter first appeared in *The Future of Broadcasting*, edited by Richard Hoggart and Janet Morgan (1982).
[1]For ready assistance in assembling material for this paper, I am grateful to Richard Hewlett and several other officers of the BBC, particularly those working in sound and written archives.

magnitude of the task puts it beyond the possibility of fulfilment.

To what extent a single set of standards is applicable to all services and all types of programme has long been a vexed question, but of one thing we can be quite certain: it is only in the most general terms that any such single set of standards could be imposed on all who come before microphone and camera. In this respect the analogies all too freely drawn between broadcasting authorities and the press are grossly false. *The Daily Mirror* and *The Times* can decide upon a 'house style' to a fair degree of detail and then impose it both upon their own staff and (through the diligent editing which the leisure of even the frenetic daily press permits) upon invited contributions from outside. Whether or not, in so doing, the press 'upholds the standards of English' – let alone feels 'a clear duty' about it – is of course another matter. My point is that the press undoubtedly has the means in a way and to a degree denied to broadcasting.

In the early days of the medium, when everything transmitted was scripted, the analogy was close enough. Only in pronunciation could the broadcaster have gone his own way, and it was in this area that the Advisory Committee on Spoken English operated from 1926 to ensure that he did not – at least if he was one of the BBC's own broadcasting staff. Not that the preventive measures needed to be severe. Recruits to the young BBC were from the same educational (and social) background as those entering the law, medicine and the top branches of the press and civil service. They therefore 'spoke' (that is, pronounced) English in broadly the same way as their fellows in these professions – the 'Received Pronunciation' associated with the public schools and indeed with public pronouncements, whether from the Crown, the pulpit, the bench, or the ('legit') stage. All that the Advisory Committee felt it necessary to do was try to ensure consistency and to arbitrate in those cases where variation occurred within Received Pronunciation.[2] Insofar, therefore, as 'BBC English' was not a misnomer (the BBC merely coming to be the chief medium in which the public at large encountered RP), it was for the most part only a mildly engineered and regularized selection from the already existing dominant variety of English used in the leading professions.

But of course even this modest degree of direction could be

[2]The consequent neglect of lexical and grammatical aspects of presentation seriously contributed to the BBC's reputation for using 'difficult' language, and I return to this point below.

imposed only on the BBC's own microphone staff. There could never be any question of making this form of pronunciation the only English heard on the air: talks, short stories, drama and other entertainment from the earliest days were heard in a variety of regional and social accents, though of course care was taken (and while everything was scripted this was particularly easy) to control language presentation in a wider sense: the avoidance of coarseness, blasphemy and the like.

It would be fair to say, indeed, that it was in these far more pervasive areas of language – content, tone, style – that the image of a BBC manner grew up, and this came to be associated with, identified with, even determined by the cut-glass RP accents of announcers – 'BBC English': first as a *façon de parler*, then perhaps as a *façon de penser*. It was certainly convenient to have so easily referable a stick to beat the BBC with – as early as 1926:

> The BBC are determined to secure some uniformity of the English language as used in their studios. . . . Now, so long as the BBC restrict their efforts to teaching announcers how to pronounce simple Scottish place-names all will be well; but when it comes to standardizing the pronunciation of our whole mother-tongue we protest. . . . There is a danger of 'BBC English' becoming a sort of criterion. (*Glasgow Evening Citizen*, 21 July 1926)

Evidence of the BBC's embarrassment is not difficult to find. Protestations of innocently limited objectives stretch into the 1970s from the mid-1920s when they were definitively uttered by John Reith himself: 'There has been no attempt to establish a uniform spoken language' – it was merely 'desirable to adopt uniformity . . . of pronunciation to be observed by announcers' (*Broadcast English* 1, 1928).

But there can be no question that the dominance of RP within the BBC has been given an importance over the years that is out of all proportion to its relevance in the whole context of the BBC's communicative performance. In any case, the story has been so excellently told by Gerhard Leitner (especially 1979) that I may be forgiven for concentrating here on other aspects.

Reference has already been made to 'house style', and although – in relation to print – we think of this primarily in terms of language in its narrowest respects (spelling, for instance), it involves presentation rather widely. In the daily and weekly press, it concerns vocabulary choice, sentence length and other aspects of language, as well as column width, design of headlines and sub-headings, typeface, use of pictures and their relation to text, and numerous other matters. After instructing his colleagues to be sparing in the use of 'crossheads' to break up and enliven copy, Waterhouse (1979) goes on:

> The standard Mirror crosshead consists of one word, usually of no more than seven or eight characters. . . . Abstract nouns that relate to behaviour (*Sorrow, Theft, Attack*) are better than abstract nouns that don't (*Role, Magic, Nights*) and infinitely better than most concrete nouns (*Table, Coach, Lamp*). But verbs or adjectives may be better still. *Stole* is better than *Theft*, night lawyers allowing, and *Hot* is better than *Heat*.

Not only is style by no means limited to features of language (though these will remain my concern here), but equally no non-linguistic aspect of style in the media can be without reference to linguistic aspects. *The Daily Mirror*'s choice of racy stories and girlie pictures is inevitably matched by such choices in language as we have just seen being specified. So too it is to be expected that Dave Lee Travis will match his comments to the style of music he introduces on Radio 1 as radically as Colin Doran adapts himself to introducing a choral mass on Radio 3. Nor has the BBC ever been 'monotone': the same announcer in the 1930s (Stuart Hibberd) could permit himself a wide range between the sobriety appropriate for announcing the death of a king and the relative heartiness of introducing 'Saturday Night Music Hall'.[3] And whatever jokes we now make about announcers of old, dress-constrained despite their invisibility, we must recognize that the sartorial elegance of Angela Rippon or Kenneth Kendall before the camera today is equally an inalienable part of the communicative style.

But style is more than a matter of 'house' (*The Mirror* and *The Times*, Radio 1 and Radio 3): it is also a matter of medium and posture. We do not speak as we write. We choose clothes and speech for an interview with a potential employer other than for a pub crawl with friends (Quirk *et al.* 1972, 1.15 *ff*). And when we write to a person we do not know, we would be wise to appreciate that we cannot automatically depend on his complete understanding, let alone his cooperative sympathy. When there is a shared field of

---

[3]Something of this kind was the subject of an internal BBC memorandum of 1936 ('one voice . . . many styles'), referred to in Burns 1977, 26.

discourse (e.g. psychology or law), we can of course avoid some of the more obvious pitfalls of medium and posture by writing within the conventions established in the field concerned: in other words, by deliberately suppressing originality and as many traces of our personality as possible.

When we find ourselves writing for a number of different unknown people, of unknown professional interests and personal tastes, the difficulties of course increase exponentially. They became acute with the 'Gutenberg revolution', and William Caxton showed his awareness of them five hundred years ago in a well-known passage from the Prologue to the *Eneydos*. With book production no longer a matter of supplying one known customer with a known taste in manuscript style, it was necessary to effect some kind of 'meane', as Caxton called it, but with small possibility of avoiding every feature of language likely to displease someone or other. 'Fain would I satisfy every man,' he wrote, but knew it was impossible 'because of diversity . . . of language'.

Analogous problems, but still more acute, confronted 33-year-old John Reith in 1922 when he contemplated general management of the British Broadcasting Company. In opting (unsurprisingly) for a linguistic uniformity based (just as unsurprisingly) on what was perceived as the 'Best English' of the capital, Reith and his colleagues were in part merely following the reasoning of Caxton: the selection of a language form that would be understood and tolerated most widely. And despite the perennial objections to which I have referred, this has never been seriously challenged – at any rate so far as pronunciation is concerned – and indeed views like the following have been fairly generally expressed:

> For good or ill, what may be termed Southern English is understood more clearly over a greater area than even a slightly localized form of speech. Northcountry accent is not at all understood well in remote districts such as Devonshire.   (*The Yorkshire Observer*, 25 January 1943)

We may of course question this emphasis on comprehensibility: dialect-speaking comedians seem to have been understood across dialect boundaries without difficulty, and it is much more likely that the point most favouring 'Southern English' was its acceptability as the voice of prestige and authority. And indeed it seemed to Lloyd James that accents other than RP had lost their potential authority precisely through association with buffoonery – a process that has been going on for hundreds of years, as we see from *The Reeve's Tale*, let alone *Henry IV* and *Pickwick*:

> You mustn't blame the BBC for killing dialect. The Lancashire comedian has killed the Lancashire dialect, and made Lancashire for ever afterwards impossible for the production of Shakespeare. (*The Listener*, 2 March 1935)

But Reith's BBC had a further motive: to see its role not just in terms of entertainment, or even of information, but of improvement. The public was to be offered something better than it might think it liked – and the models of good taste ranged from the quality of jokes through the quality of music to the quality of language itself (cf. Burns 1977, 36). And many outside the BBC became convinced that the new access to a cultivated voice and way of talking would indeed bring about widespread imitation: a girl 'may encourage her young man to make pleasant sounds, as she stimulates him to wear more acceptable clothes' (Pear 1931, 83). Together with the careful scrutiny of scripts (with these objectives very much in view), it was perhaps the self-consciously 'uplifting' goal of the BBC that contributed more than anything else to a certain turgidness, even pomposity of style that even today – after the traumatic 1960s and Hugh Carleton Greene – is often felt to mark the BBC (as distinct, for example, from ITV).

There was a related but separate problem for radio in the matter of *posture*. Limited analogies again occur with print. When a writer knows (or hopes) that he is going to be read by many, does he address them as intimate friends, respected strangers, avid pupils? As dependents, as superiors? His readers may include all of these, but it is not easy to adopt a tone that is equally appropriate to them. And should he address them en masse ('Dear Brethren'), or pretend that he is writing to an individual ('Gentle Reader')?

There is abundant evidence that, with all the very real ambitions to reach out to and 'improve' the least affluent and the least privileged, the BBC addressed itself predominantly to the middle class – the people, after all, with whom the BBC staff could most realistically identify. C. A. Lewis, Reith's deputy organiser of programmes, listing in the *BBC Handbook 1928* the factors that distracted listeners' attention, included the maid entering with coffee (Black 1972, 18). Though the sights seem to have been drastically lowered in recent years, radio and television are still unable to focus upon particular consumer groups of predictable economic standing or political orientation (as can writers for the daily press)[4] and so vaguely aim at a 'middle range' (Glasgow University Media Group 1976, 68*f*).

And within this middle range, the principle was early established of pretended address to an indiviual person, isolated by his headphones or – later – within earshot of a 'loudspeaker', in a frequently darkened drawing room. A note from the Artistic Director in July 1924 (cf. Leitner 1979, 34) reads:

> The mental attitude that you are performing to a vast unseen audience is, I feel, the wrong one to adopt. It is not mob psychology for which you have to cater but the psychology of the individual.

The stylistic correlates of this in personal warmth and directness seem to have worked in some types of programme (A. J. Alan, for example) better than with others, such as the news. But in any case the format of some programmes demanded that the individual be made to feel part of a large listening community – sometimes a worldwide one. Laurence Gilliam's Christmas Day 'hook-up' of 1939 contained such gestures as the following:

> London calling[5] . . . across the wild Atlantic, . . . to the great cities and white prairies of Canada, across the North and South Pacific . . . London calling across the oceans of the world.

'The style,' as Black says (1972, 91) 'seems high-flown now, but it didn't then' – a significant comment from so informed an observer in that it draws attention both to the changed style and posture of the BBC today (still able to walk with kings, but adding a lot more of the common touch), and to the corresponding change in our attitudes and tastes as listeners.

In discussing medium earlier, our focus was upon the selection of a form of English suitable to a mass listening audience. But of course 'medium' in the broader sense (radio as distinct from print, video as distinct from audio) is bound to demand and may additionally engender medium-specific conventions of presentation with their own linguistic correlates. To take an obvious point: the eye alone can see what is the beginning and what is the ending of a newspaper article; on radio (and to a lesser extent on television), beginnings and

---

[4]Though 'generic programming' from the late 1960s went some way to 'solving' this problem – and creating new ones: cf. *Future of Broadcasting*, 82*ff*.
[5]A formula still remembered in the title of the monthly magazine of the World Service.

endings must be made orally explicit: 'This is the National Programme. Here is the weather forecast . . .'; 'BBC Radio Four. A Book at Bedtime . . .'; 'And here we are, back in the Royal Festival Hall'. As can be seen from these examples, the conventions lead to the establishment of formulae, some of which (especially those most neutral in tone) may remain in currency for long periods while others are flexibly responsive to changes in general style with the passing of time, or to differences related to types of broadcast. Rohdenburg (1973) discusses the interesting range from 'And that concludes this edition . . .' to 'And that, I'm afraid, is about all we've time for' or 'Well, that winds up our First Sports Forum.' Even the use of demonstratives is formulaic, and Rohdenburg quotes a letter from the BBC in 1970 explaining that

> 'And this brings to an end . . .' would hardly ever be used unless 'this' was still going on while the announcer was speaking. Normally, 'that' refers to an item which has just ended.

Endemic, of course, in programme announcements, medium-specific formulae and style clichés seem otherwise to be most noticeable in the presentation of news, where their development over the years (for example, in providing verbal linkage between news items, another feature scarcely known in the printed press) has shown dramatic change and where indeed the entire style of presentation has shifted most radically. This is in part inevitable, since responsibility for the news changed fundamentally from the early days, when the BBC merely gave out what the agencies offered (and duly credited them with the copyright) to the establishment of the BBC's own news investigation service. Less inevitably, the role of presenter changed too: from, at first, a totally impersonal and unidentified voice (fitting enough for material 'by' agencies outside the BBC and fitting enough for the impersonal language style of this material), to self-credited voices ('Here is the news and this is X reading it'),[6] and later still to the increasing suggestion that the presenter is *telling* us the news and not just reading it. This is hinted at in the pen seen in the presenter's hand for some news presentations – suggesting that the presenter has prepared his own notes – and more than hinted at in others by the use of a lense-located 'autocue' to disguise the fact that the presenter is reading the material (in sharp contrast to the equally

[6]From 1940; this is usually said to result from wartime security needs, but cf. Black 1972, 94.

conventional insistence in some other countries that the news be given greater authority than the presenter's by ensuring that he is *seen* to be reading a formal script). And Angela Rippon's terminal formula is 'That's it from me', a style that is a far cry not only from the linguistic formality but from the absence of personal responsibility in 'That is the end of the news'.

Since the direction of stylistic change in handling the news seems to be fully congruent with – indeed conveniently representative of – stylistic change in the BBC's output as a whole, it may be useful to compare two broadcasts more than 30 years apart. In both cases, the text represents an attempt to reconstruct the script based solely on a transcription of the version as heard over the air and nothing is known about the extent (doubtless very little, if at all, in the first case) to which the presenters departed from the script in front of them.

The first is a news broadcast of 5 February 1938, read (anonymously) by Alvar Lidell:

> Here is the third news. Copyright reserved.
>
>   The changes in Germany in the control of Armed Forces and of foreign policy fill columns in the international press today. The French papers, as well as the German and Italian, are agreed
> 5 on one point: that the changes mean a very large extension of the control of the Armed Forces, by the Nazi party. And this, needless to say, is enthusiastically welcomed in the German and Italian press. It causes grave misgiving in France. It is only necessary to quote a few sentences from one German paper to
> 10 give an idea of the official reaction throughout the German press. The *Lokalanzeiger* says, 'The uniting of the supreme military leadership in the Leader's own hands will undoubtedly accelerate the process of welding the Party and the Armed Forces together. The Party represented by its head, the Leader,
> 15 and the Army represented by its Supreme Commander, also the Leader, have been knitted together in the person of Adolf Hitler. How ridiculous therefore must the silly talk in the foreign press appear about disharmonies and alleged differences of political outlook.' Signor Mussolini has sent a telegram of congratulation
> 20 to Herr Hitler expressing great satisfaction at his assuming the effective command of all the Armed Forces of Germany. Signor Mussolini says that this will strengthen the comradeship between the armed forces and the regimes of Italy and Germany.

Herr Hitler, in his reply, says he will consider his task to
25 strengthen further the political and ideological relations which
already exist between Germany and Italy. Signor Mussolini has
also sent telegrams of congratulation to Baron von Neurath on
becoming head of the new secret Cabinet Council, to Herr von
Ribbentrop on becoming Foreign Minister, and to Field Marshal
30 Göring on becoming Field Marshal Göring. The new Field
Marshal is reported already to have taken the opportunity of
wearing his new Field Marshal's uniform. He wore it today when
he opened a private exhibition of the Academy of Arts in Berlin.
The reactions in France to the changes may be summed up by a
35 quotation from *Le Journal*. 'Control of the army,' it says,
'henceforth becomes entirely dependent on the Nazi party which
is now supreme and undis- undisputed master and the great and
only victor of the days of crisis. Generals who have thought they
could exercise influence, even though indirectly on the policy of
40 the Reich . . . who had only lukewarm faith in the military
worth of the new Italy, and who moreover found that the
Spanish affair had already lasted too long, these generals are
beaten by the Party, which imposes its ideas and which knows
only one foreign policy: that of Herr Hitler. The appointment of
45 Herr von Ribbentrop is more than abundant proof of this and
gives a stinging denial to those who proclaimed the Rome-Berlin
axis is shaken.'

In Vienna, the German news has also caused misgiving, but
hope is felt there that the new Cabinet Council may have a
50 moderating influence on German foreign policy. There have
been several rumours about the retired Commander in Chief of
the Army, General Von Fritsch, that he was or had been under
arrest and that he had been removed because of his relations
with the French army command.

The second is a news broadcast, also on sound radio, of 3 January
1972, the 'upgrading' of the presenter made manifest not merely by
his being named but by his being actually presented by an
announcer:

Announcer: Eight o'clock on Monday, the third of January,
and here's the news, from Brian Hudson.
Hudson: The headlines this morning:- Northern Ireland: Troops
battle with a crowd at a Belfast club. Malta: abuzz with rumour

5 as a Libyan plane flies in with forty men. Vietnam: President
Nixon says Hanoi must negotiate or the Americans will keep a
force there. A New York gang clean out the strong boxes of a
Fifth Avenue hotel.

First, Northern Ireland, and a pitched battle early this
10 morning at a social club in Belfast. Two civilians and one soldier
were slightly hurt as a crowd of people barricaded inside fought
to keep out troops who'd gone to the club to check who was
there. From Belfast, Chris Drake.

Drake: There were nearly two hundred men and women in the
15 Saint Mary's Hall club, which is just off the York Road, in Cause
Lane, when the army cordoned off the area and began their
operation soon after ten o'clock last night, then told the
management they intended carrying out a check on all the
people present, and within an hour seventy-four had left
20 peacefully. The rest remained inside. They barricaded the doors
and windows with billiard tables, chairs and other furniture,
and refused to leave. It was a couple of hours later, when
repeated appeals by the army had failed, that men of the Second
Fusiliers began trying to break the doors down. They were met
25 by a barrage of bits of broken furniture, bottles, glasses, billiard
balls and cues, and for half an hour the pitched battle
continued. . . .

Hudson: Next, Malta. About five hundred and fifty troops are
now known to be on stand-by in Britain in case they're needed to
30 help in the evacuation from the island. . . . Our defence
correspondent understands there are no firm plans at present for
flying any of the men out to Malta, but they will be needed there
if the troops stationed on the island find themselves having to
prepare for evacuation without the help of civilian employees.
35 Now, with details of the latest situation in Malta, our
Commonwealth correspondent, Jim Biddulph.

Biddulph: The flood of rumours connected with the British
withdrawal were given a massive boost here last night when a
Hercules transport plane of the Libyan air force landed at the
40 airport. It is said to have unloaded about forty personnel plus
cargo. . . .

At about the same time as the second of these broadcasts, the BBC
was conducting a fairly extensive investigation into the public reception of its news. A 'formal, serious, humourless and establishment

image' was found to result in part from 'unnecessary complexity of language, and a stiffness and formality in presentation' (Glasgow University Media Group 1976, 5*f*). If this verdict was applicable to picture-assisted news on BBC TV (and it is endorsed by the Glasgow Group's own findings: *ibid.*, 27), how much more so must it have applied to such material as that exemplified above in the 1938 broadcast? Quite apart from the amount of time devoted to the item and the startlingly trivial degree of detail (Göring wearing his new uniform 'today when he opened a private exhibition of the Academy of Art in Berlin'), the lexical and syntactic texture is essentially that of print, indeed of the *small* print found in the 'quality' newspapers of the day. This can be seen in comparing the style of the matrix material with that of the translated inserts from the German and French press. These are, if anything, livelier and more readily comprehensible to the ear than the embedding discourse prepared in the BBC itself for the ear alone: 'expressing great satisfaction at his assuming the effective command of all the Armed Forces of Germany', 'hope is felt there that the new Cabinet Council may have a moderating influence on German foreign policy'.

But whether we have translated quotation or BBC text, the whole is read by one single, cultured voice, the abstract, unimaginative, monotone dullness matched by a monotone, impersonal remoteness in the reading (cf. Crystal 1975, 91), with only one sign of human frailty as Lidell 'fluffs' the word *undisputed*. At the same time, we should note how rudimentary are the medium-determined conventions (virtually nothing beyond the opening formula, 'Here is the third news'), and how unlikely that listeners would have raised the kind of objections familiar in more recent times ('sloppy' colloquialism, media clichés and mannerisms). The vocal and the literate who liked the style of *The Times* would find little fault with the news on radio.

With all this, the 1972 example is in stark contrast. In so far as we are reminded of the press, it is now *The Mirror* rather than *The Times* ('abuzz with rumour', 'pitched battle'), and indeed a reminder of the press is inescapable. The device of press headlines has been adopted, with a metaphorical extension of the term itself and with imitation of the style and grammar concerned – notably in the use of the present tense ('troops battle', 'Nixon says'). Press journalism seems also to be influencing presentation in the device of sequential expansion. The few words on Northern Ireland in the 'headlines' are slightly expanded in lines 8–11, with significant lexical repetition for endorsement (*battle*, *club*, *crowd*, *troops*); the insert that follows from Belfast (lines 00 *ff*) is not only a further expansion but is a full repetition of what we have already been told twice.

But clearly we are not offered a replica of popular press style as directly as the 1938 excerpt replicated the style of 'quality' papers. Broadcast news has adapted press devices to the needs of the specific medium and has developed others in addition. Headlines in a paper are not grouped at the beginning but are distributed along with the news items that they summarize; and they are generally briefer than those broadcast, as well as being stripped of grammatical devices like articles and auxiliaries.

The self-confidence of broadcasters in evolving their own stylistic strategies can be seen in the way headlines themselves involve the sequential expansion I have mentioned. A superordinate 'heading' in the form of a verbless clause ('Northern Ireland') is characteristically followed by a brief sentential 'headline' summarizing the news item concerned: 'Troops battle with a crowd . . .'. A related and still more striking characteristic is the way in which such a superordinate verbless heading (usually a noun phrase) is then formally coordinated by *and* with the expansion concerned, even though no coordination in the grammatical sense is possible. This stylistic cliché occurs in line 0, and is a daily commonplace: 'The Olympic games and most athletes are determined to take part.'

The verbless clause (along with short, snappy sentences and the colloquial contractions like *here's* that were once conspicuously absent from news reading) contributes prominently to the new free-wheeling, breezy style of presentation. 'Eight o'clock on Monday'; 'The headlines this morning'; 'Next, Malta'. It is perhaps especially notable in the formulae used to introduce inserts, such formulae themselves characterised by preposed adverbials: 'From Belfast, Chris Drake'; 'With details of the latest situation . . . Jim Biddulph'. Before this type of insert became so common, far more explicit and deliberate switching was used: 'Now we go over to our X correspondent in Y' (with nonetheless a medium-specific metaphor in *go over*).

These presentational devices are, of course, interactive. The inserts, obviously unnecessary in any strict sense, are believed to convey immediacy and authenticity. But immediacy also demands a certain colloquialism and an avoidance of the impression that time has been available to endow a careful, literary style. And if colloquialism is therefore a desideratum, a careful consistent pronunciation and elocution can no longer be. Given indeed the dominance of inserts from a variety of far-flung speakers who obviously cannot be subjected to detailed linguistic control, it would be disturbing if there were too obvious a stylistic contrast between these and the studio-based presenters. The same arguments reduce – to say the least – the need to insist on strict RP accents. As in the Germany of the 1930s, so in the UK of the 1980s, 'Rundfunksprache ist kein phonetisches Problem, sondern ein stilistisches' (Leitner 1980, 22).

I am not of course suggesting that all stylistic devices on radio and television are thus logically purposive. As with cliché in general, many of them result from lack of time and lack of care, as journalists take the easy well-worn path to provide a hurried 90-second stretch of oral 'copy'. There is for example the over-use of the cleft sentence to provide little-wanted focus upon time adverbials, as in line 22: '*It was* a couple of hours later . . . *that* men . . . began . . .'. So also, in the six o'clock news of 13 October 1971, an insert by Tom Bostock: '*It was* early this morning *that* journalists . . . were taken . . . to the scene . . .'.

But in general the stylistic changes are both medium-determined and conscious. To a great extent they are deliberate responses to a pervasive democratization in our society as a whole, a recognition that 'broadcasting must be part of the democratic tree and all broadcasters must realize that they are sitting on one of its branches' (Hearst 1979, 14). Already in the 1960s, Hugh Carleton Greene was pointing out that a proper relationship between broadcasters and the public 'cannot exist if the language in which they are talking, and the assumptions they are making, seem to be too remote from the language and assumptions of the audience and of the times in which they are communicating' (quoted in Burns 1977, 152).

But the problems here are legion. The audience must inevitably talk a wide range of language, the details of which are little known to linguists let alone to BBC production staff. Nor are the audience's assumptions readily known: they have themselves to be assumed, with a corresponding (if fairly safe) assumption that the assumptions are spectrally ranging. What will be seen in some sectors of the population as a timidly belated response to changes in thresholds, tolerances, sensibilities will be resented by other sectors as enforcing an unacceptable pace of change – and in directions that are equally resented. For many people, the BBC's recently acquired air of derring-do seems as unrepresentatively dirigiste as the Reithian concept of giving audiences 'what they ought to want' – though it is precisely against the remnants of such a policy that the new style has been directed.

The simple polarity of 'hieratic' and 'demotic' has thus only limited application in a complex society such as our own. The BBC's hieratic style of fifty years ago was the easier for broadcasters to use since – with their education and background (Burns 1977, 98*ff*) – it was fairly natural for them and hence close to a demotic. But the new demotic stance in Broadcasting House and Television Centre is only in the most general terms closer to the speech perception and performance of the population at large – and hence it can be widely received as quasi-hieratic. The result has been to attract attacks from different sections of the population on quite different aspects of presentational style.

We have had, for instance, predictable tirades against what is seen as the new sloppiness ('this strata', 'infer' for 'imply', and the like). There was deemed to be such 'wide public concern about the standard of spoken English on the BBC' in 1979 that Aubrey Singer intervened for management and invited a month's surveillance of output. In the event, the trio of observers found little enough to upset them and were equally unimpressed by the evidence of wide public concern or the sources of complaint: 'all the letters were written by middle-aged or by elderly people' (Burchfield *et al.* 1979, 8). Although this point does not of itself invalidate the complaints (even the most youthful members of a society are sometimes wrong), the experience of the observers matches that of the Annan Committee who received rather few protests about 'poor English' (*Future of Broadcasting*, 247).

More serious has been the way in which people have felt alienated by the tones of easy sophistication that have accompanied the trend to informality. Such people have included the black and brown immigrants who can feel excluded at best and – worse – can suspect that they are being slighted. And they have included large numbers of the working and lower middle class who – whatever their own standards are in private talk – are easily offended by breaches of linguistic convention in the media (a point significantly respected by even the most scandal-oriented sections of the public press). 'Some are outraged by what to them are blasphemous expletives; others by sexual or scatological words' (*Future of Broadcasting*, 258). Standards in these matters are not nearly as volatile as the avant-garde would like to think, but they are nonetheless notoriously variable at any moment within a given society (cf. Chapter 2 below). It is clear that the major media, printed and broadcast alike, need to tread warily and to exercise considerable self-censorship.

And indeed they do. The danger of libel and other legal infringements have constantly to be watched. Political sensitivities demand in-house conferences to decide whether a blood-letting has involved 'terrorists' or 'nationalists' or 'freedom fighters'. Broadcasting staff must carefully interpret the law of the land in refraining from language suggestive of racial prejudice: there should be no 'welshing'. They must, indeed, go beyond the mere law in being alert to social sensibilities, respecting such movements as 'gay lib', 'women's lib' and of course religious beliefs, beyond the call of statute. As Robert Robinson has wisely said, 'The broadcaster has . . . an obligation to tread a delicate path – not under any moral obligation, but simple good manners enjoin it.' But more than good manners are involved. It takes the sharpened insights of the experienced communicator to acquire a full respect for the linguistic instrument by which man both releases his fancy and reflects his mythologies.

Thus when our society's vanguard is looking for 'inclusionary policies', broadcasters are wise to speak rather of 'the average person' than of 'the man in the street' – just as they are wise to recognize that 'claiming responsibility' with respect to IRA activity has positive and victorious overtones. This is the sort of issue that is on the agenda for the weekly meetings, for example, of the BBC's News and Current Affairs personnel, and they are among the issues that are clearly set forth for the newsmen of radio in the 70-page booklet, *BBC News Guide*. This is not, of course, to say that the existence of the 'style sheet' mentality is always advantageous. It is said that the BBC 'cocked up the assassination of President Kennedy' because it could not be readily decided whether this required the procedure for a head of state's death 'or whether it was just a crime' (Glasgow University Media Group, 80).

But although such controls exist, they are limited in extent and they are, so to say, 'defensive': they aim at protecting the BBC's interest in one way or another (whether avoiding legal action or a listener's complaint or a loss of audience). The question arises whether controls might *(a)* have a wider purview, and *(b)* have more outward-looking goals, perhaps to 'purify the dialect of the tribe' if not actually return to concepts of wholesale 'cultural therapy'.

The answer to *(a)* is in my view 'yes'. I have long regretted (though understanding the evolutionary reasons) that, alone among the linguistic performance factors, pronunciation was given such importance as to justify a special unit to provide in-house guidance. There seems in fact to have been a drastic narrowing of the concept Reith enunciated to his newborn Advisory Committee on Spoken English in June 1926, that it should help the BBC 'to stem modern tendencies to inaccurate and slurred speech' – which certainly does not suggest a restriction to issues of Received Pronunciation. Subsequently, one member of the Committee, Logan Pearsall Smith, kept returning to the need to tackle broader linguistic issues and in an undated memorandum we find him urging that they take into 'consideration not only the pronunciation but the choice and the formation of words'.[7] He seems to have been unsuccessful.

After being a member of the committee responsible for appointing a new head of the Pronunciation Unit in the summer of 1978, and hence having had an opportunity to consider the present responsibilities of the Unit (largely reduced, with the severely diminished insistence on RP, to advising on the pronunciation of names, British and foreign), I wrote to BBC management suggesting 'a broader-based unit'. Since there was now strong evidence that the public in this country (and still more abroad[8]) in my view expected 'the BBC to represent and reflect the best standards of current English' and since linguistic scholarship has furnished us with far sounder reference works on English lexicon, grammar and sociolinguistic factors in usage as a whole than were available fifty years ago, I argued that there was a good case for providing production departments with far-reaching guidelines on language and style. These guidelines would emphasize the falsity of outmoded beliefs in a single, invariant 'standard' in language as in culture at large. Catholicity, authenticity and flexibility are superior watchwords, and I have

[7] I am indebted to Professor David Abercrombie for this reference.
[8] The BBC's responsibility for ensuring a good standard of English in its World Service (especially in view of the world importance of English: cf. Jernudd and Shaw 1979) raises issues that had regretfully to be excluded from the scope of this chapter.

been impressed in discussions with trainee producers at the readiness to appreciate this.

If my answer to *(a)* is 'yes', it is because I believe in the positive influence of broadcasting services on the extended response to – and probably on the active use of – the language. It is not easy to demonstrate the truth of this; and in reaction to early naiveties on this subject (which looked, essentially, for 'social climbing' reactions in the spread of class accents)[9] it has become fashionable to deny influence entirely – on linguistic as on other aspects of behaviour. But the Annan Committee reviewed the issue in some detail and seemed to conclude (with Lord Clark) that television, for example, 'had enormously widened people's horizons; it had increased their knowledge of the world and of nature, and even whetted their appetites for art and ideas' (*Future of Broadcasting*, 24; cf. also Newby 1976) – just as no-one has seriously questioned that radio in the Reith era had extended the public's taste in music. None of this can be true without a corresponding extension of the public's sensitivity to and knowledge of language. And Fishman (1974, esp. p. 1639) has stoutly reasserted the media's influence in respect of language standards.

But a 'yes' answer to *(a)* would still not require a 'yes' answer to *(b)*, affirming that broadcasting authorities have an actual responsibility to raise the public's standards, whether in language or in anything else. It is much easier in this instance to muster arguments in favour of a negative answer. The strongest and the most obvious is that the more overt and active such a therapeutic policy, the greater would be the resistance not only from listeners and viewers but from the programme and production staff within broadcasting. The BBC could best fulfil a role of influencing for good by providing – within such obvious limits as legal constraint – free rein to its creative staff. *Preaching* what is believed to be best in language, art and culture as a whole is no job for broadcasting authorities: it is enough that they be free to *reflect* the best: the realistic, plural best.

[9]'Millions of listeners will be influenced by the way announcers speak' (*The Star*, 16 January 1940). Cf. also Pear 1931, 82*ff*. The advent of radio and then of the 'talkies' gave rise to much public discussion of voice and pronunciation – in much the same way as the advent of printing was followed by numerous treatises on orthography.

References

BBC News Guide (1975). London: BBC (mimeo).

Black, P. 1972: *The Biggest Aspidistra in the World*. London: BBC.

Burchfield, R. W., Donoghue, D. and Timothy, A. 1979: *The Quality of Spoken English on BBC Radio*. London: BBC.

Burns, T. 1977: *The BBC: Public Institution and Private World*. London: Macmillan.

Crystal, D. 1975: *The English Tone of Voice*. London: Edward Arnold.

Fishman, J. 1974: 'The Sociology of Language', in T. Sebeok (ed.), *Current Trends in Linguistics* 12. The Hague: Mouton.

Future of Broadcasting, Report of the (Annan) Committee on the (1977). London: HMSO.

Glasgow University Media Group 1976: *Bad News*. London: Routledge and Kegan Paul.

Hearst, S. 1979: 'Has "Public Service Broadcasting" a Future?'. *Encounter* (May), 10-19.

Jernudd, B. H. and Shaw, W. D. 1979: *World Maps of Uses of English and Other Languages of Wider Communication*. Honolulu: East-West Center (mimeo).

Leitner, G. 1979: *BBC English und der BBC: Geschichte und Soziolinguistische Interpretation des Sprachgebrauchs in einem Massenmedium*. *Linguistische Berichte* Papier 60, Braunschweig.

—1980: ' "BBC English" and "Deutsche Rundfunksprache": A Comparative and Historical Analysis of the Language of Radio'. *International Journal of the Sociology of Language* 20.

Newby, P. H. 1976: *Radio, Television and the Arts*. BBC: London.

Pear, T. H. 1931: *Voice and Personality*. London: Chapman and Hall.

Quirk, R., Greenbaum, S., Leech, G. and Svartvik, J. 1972: *A Grammar of Contemporary English*. London: Longman.

Rohdenburg, G. 1973: 'Rundfunkendungsschlüsse im Englischen und Deutschen'. *PAKS-Arbeitsbericht* 7, Stuttgart.

Waterhouse, K. 1979: *Daily Mirror Style*. London: Mirror Group.

Coda: Considering Your English

As yet another year draws to a close with yet another book on English usage landing accusingly on one's desk, the immediate reaction is a sinking feeling. A first riffle through ('gobbledegook', 'vogue words', 'linguistic indecorum', 'the auditory mass media') seems to confirm that, whatever line he argues, Thomas Pyles will be confirming our worst fears. For if there is no smoke without fire, English must at this moment in time be in an ongoing conflagration situation.

On 21 November 1979 a score of speakers joined in a House of Lords debate on the language, a majority of them clearly convinced that there is serious deterioration. Earlier in the month I took part in a two-day debate in California organized by the English-Speaking Union on 'The State of the Language' (and launching a book with the same title: on which, more below). An even clearer majority of the hundreds present thought it was in a very poor state indeed, and getting worse rapidly (as well they might, in the opinion of several in the Westminster debate – Lord Evans dissenting – who felt that *our* deterioration was America's, with only a brief time lag). In September there was an hour of broadcast debate from the Edinburgh Festival on whether it was the 'media' that were ruining English – a question the BBC had already thought serious enough to justify having its output monitored for a month by three independent assessors. The role of broadcasters – if not as actual arsonists, then as potential firemen using transmitters as sprinkler systems – was repeatedly stressed in the Lords. Indeed, the opening speech by Lord Kings Norton did me the honour of quoting my published faith in the BBC's power for good in the matter.

Note: This Coda first appeared as a review of *Thomas Pyles: Selected Essays on English Usage* edited by John Algeo, published in *The Times Literary Supplement* on 14 December 1979.

In several English-speaking countries, radio takes just such overt therapeutic action, and one example is worth dwelling on: the South African Broadcasting Corporation's series 'Consider Your English'. Now any visitor from this country must be struck by the English of announcers and newsreaders on the SABC. My own first impression was that, by mistake, I had tuned into the BBC's world service; my second, that the broadcaster must be a new immigrant – from a United Kingdom public school (of the 1930s). And how odd, I thought: this chap would never get a broadcasting job in Dublin, or Toronto, or Sydney, or even Wellington. Is there no sense, I wondered, of comparable linguistic identity in South Africa? Of course, on the streets of Johannesburg and Cape Town (as well as in university classrooms), the English sounds distinctively South African, just as in corresponding centres English sounds distinctively American, Australian, and Irish – but certainly less confidently and no doubt less proudly. I met only a few pugnacious souls (all of them in academic linguistics) who asserted that the model of good English in South Africa was other than the voice of SABC, a voice with standards indistinguishable from those of Mr Alvar Lidell.

A sign of strength? Of holding the line against corruption and deterioration? An alternative view that I came to take seriously when I got into SABC studios myself is that it is a sign of weakness, an admission that English has no proper roots in South Africa. SABC – so this argument goes – is run by the Nationalist government (and let us note this word 'Nationalist'), and it is government policy that the English heard is the 'best' English, the best English of *England*: a foreign language with appropriately foreign standards. By contrast with the Afrikaans-speaking Afrikaner (both terms incorporating 'Africa' and emphasizing authentic, indigenous nationalism), the English-speaking whites are referred to (and refer to themselves) as 'English'. It is easy to see this lending itself to the Nationalist orthodoxy that, like the blacks of Bantu origin, they can be justifiably regarded as unintegrated immigrants. And SABC English becomes a device for alienation. Note that the title of the series 'Consider Your English' comes over the air, of course, as indistinguishable from 'Consider You're English'. Examples of the programmes that I have heard seem to confirm this by taking British standards (usually via Fowler) as axiomatically the only ones applicable.

It is against this background that we need to study Baroness

Young's wise comments in winding up the Lords debate. We must be careful not to condemn as degenerate what can more fairly be called just 'different'. We must remember, she said, that 'English is now a multi-national language and we ourselves are increasingly a multi-cultural nation'. She clearly sees the danger that a new insistence on a single standard could have a divisive and alienating effect – the exact opposite of what its advocates would have as their goal. And this is essentially the message we get from the defence of diversity in Thomas Pyles.

Many of us believe that we can best uphold standards, and improve them, by developing a wider respect for *multiple* standards. Well-chosen words in well-constructed sentences do not entail fore-going loyalty to one's social or regional group; still less do they mean affronting the individual's sense of his own style. At the same time, with the responsibilities now carried by English as a world language, we must recognize that – beside a richly variable 'demotic' – there is a vital role for a 'hieratic' that transcends social and political frontiers. To a large extent, we have this already in the world-wide English of *print*, where you can consider your English without for a moment considering you're English.

Even – though this is getting harder – without considering you're American. In *The State of the Language* (edited by Christopher Ricks and Leonard Michaels), a poem by Gavin Ewart satirizes the alleged inflation of the language in America and deplores the way we eagerly follow:

> But most terrible of all is how stupidly and dopefully
> they use (and we use) that ubiquitous 'hopefully'.

The point is predictably reiterated in the same book by Kingsley Amis, who called it the most 'denounced import to the UK in living memory until Japanese motorcars came along'. And if it is America that all the horrors are coming from, there is not much chance of stifling them at source, according to the columnist John Simon. He sees 'The Corruption of English' (the title of his essay) as stemming from 'a growing majority' of teachers in America who wilfully dis-courage good writing and standard usage.

All rather depressing, if not terrifying, and it is something of a relief to get things into perspective with the help of Thomas Pyles, who at 74 has a lifetime of teaching and scholarship under his belt.

He is able to recall his American youth when 'The hapless moppet of my day who was so lacking in grammatical self-inspection as to ask, "Miss Fidditch, can I be excused?" was, unless his condition seemed very desperate indeed, required to mend his grammar before the requested permission for relief was granted.' It is presumably part of John Simon's belief in a *trahison des clercs* that Miss Fidditch would now speed her charges to the can despite the *can*.

'Whatever the New Year holds, it holds nothing new.' Doubtless we can say this of doom-laden voices proclaiming that the end of English is at hand. But although – equally – there is nothing new in the Pyles volume (the *Selected Essays on English Usage* are reprinted from sources up to 34 years old), the sense of doom is absent. The items are presented by John Algeo, the editor of *American Speech* (what other sort is there, grumbled the House of Lords), and in a useful if oddly Latin-peppered foreword he provides a commentary on the essays and their theme, 'a view of change and continuity in the English language' – the one deplored, the other ignored 'by many self-appointed guardians of the language' in 'the murky realm of lay linguistics'.

Many of the essays were written before the recent anxiety (hysteria, some would say) about literacy and linguistic standards on both sides of the Atlantic. If the Pyles view seems somewhat anodyne in consequence, its sanely cooling effect is greatly needed. Not least for the historical perspective. We have been through deeper controversy and doubt before, and it has not deprived us of a rich, sinewy, vibrant English today, sprung anew, Phoenix-like, as Eliot said, 'from its own ashes', and now used by more writers, who reach a wider readership, than ever before.

2 Sound Barriers and *Gangbangsprache*

There is always a temptation to think that the issues of one's own time are somehow special – maybe unique. Relativistic training then makes us lean over backwards to see that every age has been confronted by remarkably similar issues.

So it is with language. We swing between feeling (even as linguists) that things are going on today that are virtually unprecedented in linguistic history and dismissively asserting (especially as linguists) *plus ça change, plus c'est la même chose*. When the Germanic peoples were Christianized, English, Scandinavian and German became imbued with Christian lexicon which was the ready springboard for entirely new metaphors. When Japan was opened up in the nineteenth century, thought and language speedily became flooded with industrial and mechanical ideas. Within the present century, we have seen English (and virtually all other languages) responding with similar immediacy to the mental technology of Freud. In these respects nothing that we see in current English is more than *la même chose*. Different ideas are hailed as 'new' with each passing generation, they are absorbed into our systems, and we excitedly match 'new' language to the 'new' notions.

But we may be forgiven if – even as linguists – we are tempted to think that recent developments are a bit more than a bit more of the same old thing.

In many ways, modernism resembles in its iconoclastic impact the Renaissance and the Reformation – a new 'dispersal of shared beliefs'. There has been a spate of philosophical, political and critical-isms – frequently in mutual contradiction, calling in question the entire basis of our society and its already uneasy sense of its values.

To grow up in a society where Laura Nauder (as right-minded

Note: This chapter first appeared in *The State of the Language*, edited by Leonard Michaels and Christopher Ricks (1980).

British might say) is liable to be despised might be expected to result in an absence of firm ideas on what is to be admired. And we must recognize that this is exactly how it seems to a fairly large number of people: the type of people for whom Joseph McCarthy spoke in the 1950s and for whom (on a different wavelength) Mary Whitehouse speaks today. To the silent majority (at least allegedly a majority, and actually not all that silent), liberalism begat permissiveness which in turn begat a fashionably rigid orthodoxy. One may (becoming must) be permissive about issues once decently outlawed: adultery, homosexuality, the extreme left, women's rights, blacks' rights. One may not be permissive about issues once regarded as reasonably respectable: colonialism, anti-Semitism, the extreme right, men's rights, whites' rights. Anyone might in fact be pardoned for suspecting a mindlessly perverse inversion of norms. All very confused and confusing.

But the young or at any rate the pacesetters have not been particularly confused. They have shown a rather consistent sense of direction, and clear ideological norms seem to have emerged. These can be summed up broadly as (a) a concerned sympathy for others, particularly the perceived underdog; (b) a contempt for hypocrisy; and (c) an existential determination to explore human experience to the fearless limits of individual need. This is not how everyone sees things, of course, and I shall have something to say later about the very real abuses and perversions.

The linguistic reverberations of all this are as sharply palpable as the social ones. Sensitivity to the other guy shows up in the welcome proscription of racially disparaging labels – *hun, wop, wog, yid* and the like. No little nigger boys sit upon a wall – and even the chummy *my boy* is avoided by the more discriminating if the chum is black; a British minister gets into trouble because he says he hates 'welshing'; we learn to be careful about saying 'a man' where a woman could justly feel excluded. Or just 'you,' – 'The thing about ball points is that they make you careless about your handwriting: not you, I mean – anyone.' Here is language as it ought to be, one feels: pliably responsive to human feelings.

There is no serious antipathy to this 'social concern' trend: merely some scepticism as to its value, some sneering at what are seen as its pretensions, and some raucous jesting at the wit-level of 'personi-pulate'. Nor has there been much opposition to the second trend, exposing hypocrisy: explicit opposition there could scarcely be. The idols of 'participation', 'open government' and the like could scarcely be worshipped without acknowledging at least the existence of homosexuals, the wife-swappers, the homeless, the censored, the tax refugees, and other groups that convention, cowardice or guilt may prompt us to ignore. Linguistically, this has meant for instance despising pussyfoot titillation by evasive euphemism accompanied by the knowing wink, the conspiratorial giggle: the smut of the music hall, Chuck Berry and his 'ding-a-ling', sexual innuendoes conveyed by *it*, *do*, *thing*: it was this style of 'good clean fun' that earned contempt. It came to be widely felt that linguistic concealment was itself obscene. And if all this promoted the urge to call a bowel movement a shit and a colored gentleman a black, it was just another aspect of the reluctance to call a spade a nigger.

The exploring of human experience, and using language to match, has roused more feeling: not surprisingly, since the effects have been far more remarkable; and the extent to which we have moved from Victorian standards is little short of startling. Dickens began *Oliver Twist* in the same year that Victoria began her reign, and in his preface to the third edition (1841) he discusses public reaction to the book – reaction, at any rate, 'in some very high moral quarters' where it had seemed 'coarse and shocking' that 'some of the characters . . . are chosen from the most criminal and degraded of London's population; . . . that the boys are pickpockets and the girl is a prostitute.' In other words, offence was taken on the grounds of *content*, and in defending himself vigorously (with appeals to Gay, Hogarth, and Fielding) Dickens made the point that he had been careful to ensure propriety in respect of *expression*. 'No less consulting my own taste, than the manners of the age, I endeavoured . . . to banish from the lips of the lowest character I introduced, any expression that could by possibility offend.'[1]

A century later, 'the manners of the age' were not vastly different. In the preface to his poetic and impressionistic memoir, *In Parenthesis* (London 1937), David Jones regretted that in describing the horrors and obscenities of war he had been 'hampered by the convention of not using impious and impolite words.' He used several that Dickens denied himself (*bloody*, *bugger*, *arse*, *shit*, for

[1]*Oliver Twist*, ed. K. Tillotson (Oxford 1966), lxi, lxiv. Although *The Quarterly Review* in 1837 marvelled at Dickens's having captured (in *Pickwick*) the 'unadulterated vernacular idioms of the lower classes', a critic in the same journal two years later more aptly praised him for the linguistic 'dilution' and for wrapping up the oaths of Bill Sikes in 'silver paper'.

example; *you prize Maria Hunt, effing,* and *efficacious*
– elaborately annotated), and would have been happy to defend the
inclusion of more (save 'blasphemy in any theological sense' – a
point to which we shall return) because of his conviction that they
gave to the speech of his fellow victims 'a kind of significance, and
even at moments a dignity'. Sometimes in fact their use 'under
poignant circumstances' could produce 'real poetry'.

So, still the disjunction of experience and expression. But between
these two dates, 1837 and 1937, a great deal had of course happened – notably *Ulysses* and D. H. Lawrence. The fuss over *The
Rainbow* (1915) was on the grounds of content, but with *Lady
Chatterley* content was obtrusively and inalienably tied to language:
just how inalienably we can see by comparing the expurgated
version of 1928 with the unabridged version which could achieve a
London publication only in 1960 – and then amid outcry and court
proceedings.

For the 1950s were little more liberated than 1937 and 1837. When
Herman Wouk's novel of the other 'great' war, *The Caine Mutiny*,
was published in 1951, the author noted in his preface (whether in
apology or pride is not clear) that 'the general obscenity and blasphemy of shipboard talk have gone . . . unrecorded.' Interestingly,
The Sunday Times recommended the novel explicitly because it
abjured 'conscientious obscenity' (the choice of 'conscientious' is
significant: the backlash beginning before real permissiveness had
been felt), and *The Times Literary Supplement* actally praised it for
the 'realistic atmosphere'.[2] Even travelling with Charley in 1960,
John Steinbeck could find (extraordinarily) nothing more serious
happening to the language than the destruction of 'localness' by the
'package English' delivered by the media, sad even if the result was
'perhaps better English than we have ever used'.

It is against this background that we can perhaps see the 1960s and
1970s in perspective – see how far we moved in how short a time,
from the agonizing over *Lolita, Lady C, Last Exit* to Kurt Vonnegut,
Erica Jong and Martin Amis, making footsteps for his father to
follow.

But we must not get fixated on the reception of contemporary
fiction. At least as striking is the way writers have shifted their
linguistic stance in a more pervasive way. 'My English text is chaste,'

[2]The two reviews nearly replicate the contradictory attitudes of *The Quarterly
Review* mentioned in footnote[1] above.

wrote Edward Gibbon autobiographically, 'and all licentious passages are left in the decent obscurity of a learned language.' As in the eighteenth century, so in the first half of the twentieth. When I was a child, it was normal for translations of the more entertaining 'classics' to leave in the original the juicily salacious bits – on the theory, I used to suppose, that for all their huffing and puffing, editors never really expected us to master the languages we were supposed to be learning. Or that those who had traded their adolescent energies for philological accolades could have no grounds for complaint – including Portnoy's.

Not long ago, I compared the commentary on *The Summoner's Tale* that we find in the 1957 Harvard edition (for university students) with the London edition of 1975 aimed at girls and boys in (high) school. The guide who takes the friar on his tour of hell says to Satan:

> Shew forth thyn ers, and lat the frere se
> Where is the nest of freres in this place!

The Harvard editor, doubtless glad to hide his blushes behind the screen of Middle English spelling, can bring himself to mention the point only periphrastically: a 'repulsive conception' also represented, he says, in pictorial art of the time. The British editor of 1975 chats amiably in his notes of 'Satan's arse' and grapples with the central bawdiness with frank confidence.

Sex and scatology, all right. David Jones would have defended such explicitness; but blasphemy is quite another thing. 'Quite obviously,' he says, 'that is all I would consider' as being beyond the pale. Clearly, there is still a good deal of feeling in support of this view. Witness, for one thing, Anthony Burgess's obvious awareness of daring in his concern with G. G. Belli (born in the same decade as Keats) both in *Abba Abba* and *Beard's Roman Women*. When *Gay News* published James Kirkup's poem 'The Love that Dares to Speak its Name' in June 1976, a prosecution ensued, not on the grounds of the necrophily nor of the (rather mildly) obscene language but of the blasphemy involved in attributing active homosexuality to Christ. The case was successful and the verdict conferred a (suspended) prison sentence.

But if this was significant, the storm of protest over the verdict was at least equally so. It was made abundantly clear that offending God was for many people a great deal less offensive than offending a woman job applicant, an Asiatic immigrant – or a writer's white-hot sense of freedom. This is the ironic climax of the Lawrentian puritanism to which Richard Hoggart drew attention in the *Lady Chatterley* lawsuit, back in what now sometimes seems the Middle Ages.

The defiantly repeated attempts in our time to endow God with sexuality are strictly parallel to the age's implicit insistence on the godhood of mankind. The wheel of anthropomorphism has turned full circle, the deification of *Homo sapiens* coinciding with unisex – the concept, like the word, reflecting the will to see something deeply common to man and woman. In this context the flagrant exposure – pictorial and linguistic – of sexuality is not unlike the outward display at voluptuous Hindu Konarak: the will to recognize that our thought and language have traditionally exaggerated, by hiding, what can be seen as commonplace biological facts when they are openly paraded.

Here is where I see my tripartite trend (social concern, rejection of hypocrisy, the frank exploration of experience) as essentially unitary. The three aspects can be seen coming together, for instance, in women's lib. Equal opportunity, 'affirmative action', bra burning, resistance to sexploitation in advertising – with their linguistic correlates in *Ms, chairperson*, the hunting down of covert claims to male supremacy (as in *Stone Age Man* or the excessive use of masculine pronouns and of male characters in children's literature) are strictly congruent with the liberation of the female as a lover: the right to orgasm by whatever agency and through whichever organ the individual pleases, the right to sexual initiative, and so on. These in turn of course have their linguistic correlates, as in the verb *fuck* being able to take a plural subject and an unexpressed reciprocal object, like *kiss* ('we kissed' equaling 'we kissed each other') or even – again like *kiss* – to take a feminine subject as readily (according to Erica Jong) as a masculine.

But in any case the trend is one that is part of a quite long-established movement away from old constraints and rigidities. Democratization and a limbering up in social mores are plainly rooted in Victorianism itself, and significant linguistic reflexes are not difficult to find. They are prominent, for example, in the insistence by the Fowler brothers that simple is beautiful and that the short 'Anglo-

Saxon' words are to be preferred to polysyllabic classicisms.[3] This tradition, strongly developed by A. P. Herbert, Ivor Brown, Eric Partridge, Ernest Gowers and others (to mention only British exponents), has resulted in marked changes in the style of white papers, nonstatutory documents, *Times* leaders, and other traditional repositories of extreme formality. One thinks too of how far the BBC has come since the early days when announcers sat reading the news, unseen, in dinner jackets and Oxford accents. One recalls that Franklin D. Roosevelt increasingly established presidential contact with his radio 'fireside chats', rather than with platform rhetoric. There has been, in fact, a rather widespread reaction against the remoter aspects of formality and the sense of rigid appropriacy. We have come to insist that the different styles of language (or dress) required for different occasions and purposes are neither immutable nor even absolutely obligatory.

Not that we have in actual fact levelled out to a 'unistyle,' of course, any more than to a unisex. One of the things that reduces Anthony Burgess's novel *1985* from horror to farce is the projected linguistic engineering. We are to envisage not merely a generalizing of substandard grammar (*I've ate it*) – which can be paralleled in many languages – but also a standardizing of a single style, fit equally for idle chatter and for translating the Declaration of Independence. Here is a sample of the 'Workers' English' version of Hamlet's 'To be' speech:

> Is it more good to get pains in your fuckin loaf worryin about it or to get stuck into what's getting [*sic*] you worried and get it out of the way and seen off?

Such a monotone language – though not inconceivable – is inherently implausible, not least because it is not easily paralleled in observable natural languages. Certainly nothing in the linguistic changes accompanying the current social revolution leads us to expect a dissolution (as distinct from a diminution) of the distinction between 'distant' (formal) and 'intimate' (informal) language, however obviously the defining characteristics of both have shifted. Even those who feel most free to sport liberated slang and obscenity readily appreciate the unacceptable mixture of tones in

Bye-bye, Your Holiness. See you!

[3]H. W. and F. G. Fowler, *The King's English* (Oxford 1906), II.

Hi, John: I'm just phoning to say your sister has croaked.

Professor Crowell, I think I understand your first two points but could you explain that last fucker?[4]

Now, of course, there are presumably folk who can say 'Bye-bye' to the pope, but they are not among those who call him (in the same breath, at any rate) 'Your Holiness'. Professor Crowell, like his student, could well have referred to a ticklish bit of some hypothesis as 'that last fucker', given the right circumstances.

And the circumstances include relations between the discourse participants.[5] The two invitations

Patrons are requested to ascend to the next floor.
Up you go, chaps!

may be paraphrases of each other but they are not interchangeable. We operate according to a delicate sense of appropriacy rules, and relations between participants are not merely convention but (again) involve social concern. It may always sound brutal to refer to death as 'croaking', but it is less brutal when used of a stranger's death than that of a friend's sister. Beside Grice's discourse maxims (be informative, truthful, relevant, clear etc.),[6] it has been pointed out that 'politeness and consideration for the feelings of one's addressee' can be overriding.[7]

This means, among other things, that one's addressee needs to know whom he is listening to:

'John's drunk, it seems.'
'Who says?'

The question is not merely to demonstrate the foregoing point but to show how easily a speech act can fail to make its authority clear: *it seems* could mean 'it seems to me' (in which case it is the speaker who 'says', in the sense of asserting John's inebriation) or 'it seems from what I can gather of other people's allegations.'

Now there is a long-standing appropriacy rule in fiction such that the narrator (the third-person narrator, that is) observes a decently

---

[4]Cf. B. K. Dumas and J. Lighter, 'Is *slang* a Word for Linguists?', *American Speech* 53 (1978), and my article 'Language and Tabu', *New Society* 44 (1978).
[5]Cf. R. Quirk, S. Greenbaum, G. Leech and J. Svartvik, *A Grammar of Contemporary English* (London and New York 1972), 23*ff.*
[6]H. P. Grice, 'Logic and Conversation', in P. Cole and J. L. Morgan, (eds.), *Syntax and Semantics* (New York 1975), vol. 3.
[7]J. Lyons, *Semantics* (Cambridge 1977), vol. 2, 593.

'distant' linguistic relation to his unseen, unknown reader, however he may 'allow' his characters to speak to each other or to themselves. 'Don't blame me,' says Chaucer, 'if you are offended by the Miller's coarse language: my job is just to repeat what he said.' Just as *Umgangssprache* is of the *Umgang*, the speech of familiars, so is *Gangbangsprache* the speech of the gang: the narrator, *qua* narrator, hesitates to soil his typewriter. Ardently preserving the stance of the archetypal narrator, even the most salacity-slanted newspapers primly cover the pubic hair of their language. Even contemporary novelists would tend to regard the first of the following as discoursally ill-formed in comparison with the second:

> Smith helped Priscilla into the car and drove off to where he had fucked her the previous week.

> 'We'll go to where I fucked you last time,' Smith thought to himself, as he helped Priscilla into the car.

But the liberal and skilful use that is now made of 'free indirect speech' has markedly diminished the distinction between narrator and narrative, in consequence tending to obliterate the linguistic constraints hitherto placed upon the narrator in relation to his reader, above all making more ambivalent what Benveniste has called 'les indicateurs de subjectivité'.[8] This is true even in first-person narratives. Does Gore Vidal himself endorse the following view of history or is it only his brilliant but far from omniscient heroine: 'the time of the Beatles, the spiritual high noon of the twentieth century' (*Kalki*)? And notice that even 'delocutive' verbs provide authority only for the substance, and authority for the expression is left equivocal:

> John claimed that he fucked her.

Is the narrator repeating John's choice of verb or is it his own paraphrase of John's claim?

In *Jake's Thing* (1978), a novel of some linguistic sophistication, Kingsley Amis ably illustrates ways in which the role of narrator can be superimposed on that of character. Jake is travelling by bus and the narrator looks through his character's sardonic eyes. Near Warren Street

---

[8]E. Benveniste, *Problèmes de linguistique générale* (Paris 1966); cf. R. Quirk, *The Use of English* (London 1968), ch. 15, and A. Banfield, 'Narrative Style and the Grammar of Direct and Indirect Discourse', *Foundations of Language* 10 (1973).

the stone face of a university building was spattered with rust-stains from scaffolding on which Jake had never seen anybody at work. Even Gr nville Co rt, Collin woo C urt . . . lofty structures of turd-coloured brick . . . seemed to be deserted. Even or especially.

It is Jake who sees (and *notices*) the decadently unrepaired signs, Jake who selects the epithet 'turd-coloured', Jake who bleakly adds the pedantic afterthought: just as it is Jake who (in passages of 'narrative') bitterly mimes other people's talk, refers to an elderly stranger as 'an old bitch', and who has frequent mental-linguistic flashbacks to the tired coarseness of army days thirty years ago. And just as it is Jake (in dialogue with his wife) who feels called upon to comment on the two senses of *fucking*

> Anyway, what is this fucking Workshop? I may say that if it's a *fucking* Workshop you can all count me out

– no gangbang for him – so too it is Jake who (in narrative) plumps for the same verb, in its nonliteral sense, though the 'indicateurs de subjectivité' are not explicit:

> He took a gulp. Although he much preferred drink with food he was fucked if he was going to, etc. 'I don't know,' he said a little wildly.

But although (like Burgess in *1985*) Amis is taking a bitterly jaundiced view of his times, he apparently sees little danger of our collapsing into linguistic uniformity. On the contrary, much of his satire focuses upon several of the traditional stylistic distinctions which polarize language use: for example, clinically pompous and euphemistic jargon for what is very differently expressed in the *Umgang*:

> . . . oh and by the way non-genital includes tits, excludes them rather, I should say breasts. No, mammary areas.

Changes in constraint mean not so much a new style as the use of an already established style in new environments. And this takes us back to the question raised at the beginning of this essay: How new are the linguistic forms we are discussing? A year or two ago in Bombay, I was asked by an Indian emeritus professor why the English language had changed so calamitously. He went on to contrast his experience at Oxford in the 1920s with his impressions on a visit made fifty years later. Whereas his memory had been of students' language being 'correct and standard', it seemed now

incomprehensible with slang, regionalisms and coarseness. I had to
tell him that in all probability everything he now heard could have
been heard fifty years ago – but less publicly and less in university
circles; that, whereas a couple of generations ago, students and dons
suppressed any urge they might feel to speak with the vernacular
frankness that they undoubtedly understood, the suppressive urges
were now if anything working in the opposite direction, with the
young fearing rather the sneers at mealy-mouthed euphemism and
even at careful pronunciation.

Put it another way. In the 1880s, George Gissing commented that
the foul language of 'the nether world' had 'never yet been exhibited
by typography, and presumably never will be.' But he must surely
have been equating 'typography' with the conventional and respectable press – just as my Indian professor was equating the English of
the 1920s with the conventional English of the conventional Oxford
type. Gissing could scarcely have been unaware of *Pearl* ('A Journal
of . . . Voluptuous Reading', whose monthly issues ran for a year or
so just a century ago) and the voluminous printed material of his
own and previous times in which such language was very fully
'exhibited' indeed. And when we look back at the style of explicitness
today, there is not a great deal that seems different ('To put my prick
in here – into your sweet cunt, and fuck you' (*Pearl*, October 1879)):
it is rather that we are now used to encountering it in social and
literary contexts from which it was once excluded. A big enough
change in all conscience, but one that is in tune with the social, moral
and philosophical changes I have postulated. Most notably, it is less
a change in language itself than in its distribution; and even the
changed distribution must not be exaggerated, largely being as
confined as ever to very intimate talk and as absent as ever from the
printed media and mass fiction.

Must not be exaggerated? Those with sensibilities recently
offended by spray-gun obscenities flagrantly unignorable on walls in
Chicago or London (or by poems like Kirkup's) may feel rather that I
have underestimated the social and linguistic changes to the point of
being dismissively complacent. I find it no easier than anyone else to
view sympathetically the abuses and perversions of what I have been
trying to see as broadly beneficent trends. Obscene and brutal
language is certainly more audible not merely among the idealistic
and 'progressive' but also among the muggers, the 'Paki-bashers',
black hoodlums and white backlashers, and it is not surprising if the

relaxed constraints are linked in the minds of many not with an enhanced democracy but with more sinister fascistic trends, street violence and mob rule. There is nothing liberal or 'liberated' in getting a thrill out of linguistic flashing at old ladies, in the hope of shocking but with the effect 'only' of terrifying. Some of the self-consciously offensive language of student revolt and the proscriptions of unfashionable subjects and speakers undoubtedly blur the distinction between the extremes of liberalism and neo-Nazism.

Nor am I unaware of the sillier extravagances and exaggerations of even the most high-minded among libbers – still less of the uneven motivation of many who have jumped on the bandwagon. Lenora Timm has drawn circumspect attention to the way enthusiasts actually damage women's lib by sloppy linguistic observation and hasty, ill-considered generalizations.[9] Worse, not only have the porn racketeers predictably cashed in on the increased freedom to exploit the titillatory and surviving shock value of quadriliteralism; so have purveyors to superficially more serious and scholarly readers.[10]

I do not ignore (still less condone) such things: I am merely asserting their lack of significance and above all the lack of evidence they provide of significant linguistic change. To take just one obvious point, graffiti, we have evidence of a vigorous tradition measured not in hundreds but in thousands of years: one can scarcely get excited by the fact that felt pen and spray gun have recently made graffiti easier to write. Certainly no change in what is apprehended as 'obscene' can be in question: otherwise, why bother to spray? And if they are now on outside walls rather than in (what Gibbon might have called) the 'decent obscurity' of (what I have certainly called) 'lewd low loos',[11] I would be inclined to chalk (or spray) this up to the antihypocrisy trend.

The porn merchants like the poor have always been with us, as have the cruel and the brutal and the mentally retarded. We must take the roughnecks with the smoothies and accept that any major social movement will spawn its deviants. All in all, I remain

---

[9]In *Lingua* 39 (1976) on R. Lakoff, *Language and Woman's Place* (San Francisco 1975). See also C. Miller and K. Swift, *Words and Women* (London 1977), and my review in *The Times Literary Supplement*, 28 October 1977.

[10]See the discussion by D. J. Enright in *The Times Literary Supplement*, 25 August 1978.

[11]'The Smut Smiths', *The Times Literary Supplement*, 19 August 1977.

convinced that the sociolinguistic health of English speakers now[12] is in better shape than when Dickens could congratulate himself on avoiding speech that might 'offend the ear' or when *The Times Literary Supplement* could praise the tight-lipped Wouk for his 'realistic' language.

[12]And not only English speakers, of course. The trends I have discussed in English (sometimes with America leading and Britain following after a discreet interval of a year or so; sometimes – as with the admission of tabu words in dictionaries – with Britain in the lead) can be paralleled in many if not most languages. In Sweden we have the recent '*du*-reform'; in Japan the immensely complex sociolinguistic constraints are weakening somewhat, with girls using certain forms traditionally the prerogative of males; in French-speaking countries, older people have had to get used to words like *bouquin* in noncolloquial contexts and to *je m'en foutisme* used in quite ordinary exasperation.

3 International Communication and the Concept of Nuclear English

International communication – an indisputable desideratum – does not presuppose, let alone prescribe, a single international language. But it has long been held as virtually axiomatic that this would constitute the ideal basis. For over a century,[1] and especially in the past quarter-century, we have come to believe that this goal is within reach, with English rating a greater world spread than any other language in recorded history. Yet within the past decade, many people have started to wonder: people concerned with international affairs in general as well as members of the profession engaged throughout the world in teaching English.

The doubts have been arising on two grounds:

(a) the degree of variation in the forms of English in use – fears, indeed, of its rapid dissolution; and

(b) the practicability – not least in view of (a) – of teaching the language, especially on a mass scale, to the level required for international usefulness, given the enormous deployment of educational resources that this demands.

The divergence between one man's English and another's is great enough to be striking (though hardly, I think, alarming) within each of the English-speaking countries. The steadfast Anglo-Saxon opposition to academy-style attempts at standardization has harmonized in recent years with an educationist's orthodoxy discouraging interference with a child's most local and intimately felt language. The absurdities of an earlier generation's preoccupation with 'correctness' have been abandoned, and in some places the

Note: This chapter first appeared in *English for Cross-cultural Communication*, edited by Larry E. Smith(1981).

[1] I am indebted to Gregory Trifonovitch for a Japanese reference of 1859 (Fukuzawa Yukichi) predicting English to be the most useful language in the world of the future.

pendulum has swung to a position where quite extreme permissiveness has been actually encouraged. Where this trend has coincided with political movements towards community identity (as with 'Black English' in the United States), counter-standard policies have become especially radical without anyone – so it seems to me – having much clear perception of the long-term implications.

Naturally, in this context, the divergence between one *country's* English and another's is seen to be in danger of growing much more seriously wide, with no common educational or communicational policy even theoretically applicable, but rather with nationalism strongly (if haphazardly and even unconsciously) endorsing a linguistic independence to match political and other aspects of independence. The voices of Australia and New Zealand and the Irish Republic (as heard for instance on the national radio) are as limited to purely intranational norms, as are those of Britain and the United States. I shall say something later of centripetal influences, not least in the name 'English' being applied confidently to all these varieties. But it would be idle to pretend that the name itself is adequate guarantee of linguistic integrity, or that the varieties of English used in Britain, America and Australia are more unified than the varieties of 'Scandinavian' used in Norway, Sweden and Denmark where each is regarded – and named – as a separate language.[2]

Diversity within English is liable to be much greater, however, and to lead to far more acute problems in those countries (such as India, Nigeria, the Philippines) where English is not a native language but nevertheless has widespread use for administrative, commercial and other internal purposes. Here, in contrast to the native English-speaking countries where the language – in whatever variety – is naturally acquired, English has to be formally taught; and here therefore the question of standards is actively and often agonizingly debated. Since the teaching has to be done by teachers who had similarly to be taught the language and who inevitably learnt it to varying degrees of adequacy, change in the acceptable standards of achievement is not surprisingly very rapid. In any case, in a vast country like India, with a long history of English for internal communication, the natural processes of language – culture interaction have produced a large number of phonological, grammatical, lexical and stylistic features that have become thoroughly imbued

[2]There are of course further internal linguistic complexities in Norway.

and arguably inalienable (cf. Kachru 1976b). Indeed, with an estimated 25 million people making regular use of the language, India is the third largest country in the world with English established as a medium for internal purposes.

It is from this that there springs (by the imperfect analogy with British English, American English and the like) the concept of recognizing Indian English as a comparable national variety with its own internal determinants of acceptability, however much it may be seen historically as largely derivative from British English (cf. Strevens 1977, 133, 140). Clearly, the range of English in India (from the pidginized dock-worker to the government clerk, to the judge, to the voice of All-India Radio) is very much greater than the nearest analogy in Britain or America – as well as sharply different in kind. Clifford Prator[3] is prominent among those who have argued that it is fundamentally unsound to encourage the recognition of non-native varieties of English. But so far as the subcontinent is concerned, the insightful researches of such specialized observers as Braj Kachru leave me convinced that it is not a matter of heresy but of accepting plain facts.[4]

Yet the facts are unquestionably daunting. We are confronted in the world by three, largely independent (and largely uncontrolled, if not uncontrollable), potentially limitless types of diversification within English. If we concede, with current educational orthodoxy, that the individual benefits by seeking community identity through contented repose in his most local variety of language, can we afford to neglect the same individual's needs in a wider role – ultimately as a 'citizen of the world'? And what can be done, in this connection, to mitigate the growing despair of the teacher with day-to-day classroom concerns – not least in the English-speaking countries themselves, but of course far more acutely in countries teaching English as

---

[3]Cf. 'The British Heresy in TESL' in J. Fishman *et al.*, *Language Problems in Developing Nations* (New York, Wiley 1968), pp. 459-76.

[4]On the basis of such facts, it is clearly a matter of internal policy for governments (in India, Nigeria and the many other countries in this position) to decide the variety of indigenized English to be taught in their education systems, weighing the immediate local needs of the many against the wider needs of those who must in addition master a form of English current in international use. It need scarcely be added that this question arises only in countries making use of English for internal purposes. Other 'national' varieties of English are of course equally discernible; but while 'Japanese English', 'German English', 'Russian English' may be facts of *performance* linguistics, there is no reason for setting them up as facts of *institutional* linguistics or as models for the learners in the countries concerned.

a foreign language and (with the present world's demands) on a mass scale?

Teaching any single one of the national varieties (say 'standard southern British' English) is a hard enough assignment. With its gargantuan vocabulary, its subtly difficult syntax, and with the recently accentuated emphasis on teaching phonetic accuracy in speech, the language is difficult enough for a specially trained native speaker to teach with small classes of highly motivated pupils. But in the vast majority of classrooms all over the world, the teacher is not a native, his English is far from perfect, his training has been seriously inadequate, his classes are by no means small, and – partly as a result of all these factors – his pupils have by no means an automatically high motivation. Add to this an examining system that is seriously at variance with classroom goals and we clearly have a potentially disastrous situation even before we grapple with the fact that the initial postulate is in doubt. Can the teacher's model be 'any single one of the national varieties'? And if so, which? And what guarantees can he (or his education authority) have of the international acceptability of that variety, now, or in fifteen years? Is the colossal allocation of national resources to the teaching of English worthwhile?

Now of course all this is to take a very black look at the black side of things. Such pessimism may be quite unjustified. Developing countries may get richer and be glad to maintain or even increase their contribution of GNP to teaching English. Better provision may be made for teacher training. Better methods of teaching English already in existence may be more widely implemented: and still better methods may yet be devised. We now have better dictionaries and grammars of English than we have ever had, and we are developing techniques for sensitizing learners to national and stylistic varieties of English and for helping them meet a predicted range of communicative needs. We are beginning to think more realistically of the goals in language learning and especially about whether it is reasonable or even responsible to seek achievement in a foreign language of all the skills we master more or less effortlessly in our native language.

Again, the diversity of English in the world may not in fact be leading to dissolution into several distinct languages. I am among many observers on record as seeing powerful centripetal, unifying forces at work, offsetting the fissiparous tendencies that local needs and nationalist susceptibilities are fostering (cf., for example, Quirk 1972 and 1978). Thanks in no small measure to a traditional spelling system which ignores the passing of the years as it transcends the vagaries of pronunciation, books and newspapers use a virtually identical English whether they originate in Bloomsbury or Baltimore, Canberra or Calcutta.[5] As regards the spoken language, too, we must not ignore the impact of radio, television, film, faster travel, and even the wide access to the same pop songs. These factors are certainly making the different varieties familiar and comprehensible to increasingly large numbers of people, and to an observable degree – as between British and American English at least – they seem to be causing productive usage to limit its variation.

But let us stay with the black side – not in any spirit of alarmist masochism but to look prudently for alternative strategies if our worst fears prove to be well-founded. What happens to English in the world (or – in due succession to English – any other language of international currency) if teaching the full language proves too costly, if new techniques of teaching turn out to be disappointing, if the natural process of language diversification effectively shatters the linguistic goal? Do we then abandon hopes for the universality of English? Do we switch to some other language in which there is less inhibition about proclaiming a single world standard? Do we abandon the democratic ideal of teaching English on a mass scale and swing instead to educating an élite small enough to make the teaching effective? Or do we abandon the idea of an international language altogether and contemplate a future of linguistic frontiers manned by faceless simultaneous translators?

It is in this context that some of us have been taking a fresh look at what linguistic theory may be able to provide. Now of course linguistics has been much involved in the turns and twists of language description and language teaching for a couple of generations, and many look upon its contributions with something less than enthusiastic gratitude. Many indeed attribute a large part of current disillusion to the intervention over the years by successive waves of brash 'experts', at one and the same time advocating doctrinaire rigour in various fashionable methodologies and squishy permissiveness in goals, norms and standards. But we need not

---

[5]It is worth noting, however, that educated or 'acrolectal' English in such countries as India achieves this universality by looking outward (in contrast to the basilects) for its standards.

throw away the bath water because we do not think the babies' faces are shining. Part of our trouble is that linguistics and the social sciences in general have remained at the data-gathering, model-building and speculative stage comparable to that of physics in the eighteenth century. In part also, no doubt, the emphasis in the current climate of opinion on environmental and cultural conservation is inhibiting our getting to the manipulating stage – manipulating the medium, that is (e.g. through planned simplification[6]), rather than only the learner. No doubt we have been rightly apprehensive of the danger of filling our green valleys with dark satanic linguistic mills. But it seems to me that the time has come to enquire whether linguistics and its sister disciplines are now mature enough to direct their insights not only to language description as hitherto but also to something more like language design.

For the purposes of this inquiry, let me ask that the following propositions be regarded as axiomatic:

(1) The world needs a single medium for international communication (*needs* is important and implies willingness to pay the price – educational, social, cultural, even financial).

(2) The possibility of a wholly new or artificially constructed 'language' has been excluded.[7]

(3) The only viable possibility is either (a) to adopt or (b) to adapt

[6]Simplification of the language, that is. Predicting failure nearly thirty years ago, George Bernard Shaw saw a way out in simplification of the teaching. In pleading for rationalization in the teaching of English as a common world language, he was ready to encourage wholesale pidginization, and thought that teachers effectively sold the pass by setting their sights too high. 'All teachers should bear in mind that better is the enemy of good enough, and perfection not possible on any terms. Language . . . should not be taught beyond the point at which the speaker is understood' (*Atlantic Monthly* 186 (October 1950), 62). This presupposes a highly simplistic view of comprehensibility, and in the context of an unrestricted and uncontrolled concept of 'English', Shaw's prescription would probably be worse than valueless. In the context of a strictly limited lexicon, however, comprehensibility – phonetic and graphic alike – becomes less of an imponderable, and at any rate many would agree with Shaw that the teacher's goal of getting his students to achieve native-like control of a foreign language is a dangerous chimera. A somewhat analogous point has been strenuously made by Professor Takao Suzuki (*Japan Times*, Tokyo, 24 June 1979), arguing (a) that it is wasteful to teach English as widely as at present in Japan, and (b) that the English taught should be a simplified form ('Englic'), based on non-native usage.

[7]Despite the ingenuity and (often) very attractive features that such inventions may display – cf. the little known Interglossa described in quite fascinating detail in a Pelican book so titled by Lancelot Hogben (Harmondsworth, 1943). Hogben's sketchy handling of modality is of some interest: see pp. 126f.

one of the world's natural languages: the starting point must be a linguistic force with existing momentum.

(4) The best current candidate for (3) is English.

Bearing in mind the black picture I have seen fit to paint, however, one further assumption is required, namely that (3a) has been tried with dismal results and prospects. I thus postulate a situation in which we are left with (3b), and I would like to explore some of the questions that would be involved in adapting English (or of course any other language) to constitute a nuclear medium for international use.

To satisfy the relevant need, 'Nuclear English' would have to possess certain general properties. It must be:

(a) decidedly easier and faster to learn than any variety of natural, 'full' English;

(b) communicatively adequate, and hence a satisfactory end-product of an educational system; and

(c) amenable to extension in the course of further learning, if and as required.

Communicative adequacy is to be understood as providing the learner with the means of expressing, however periphrastically, an indefinitely large number of communicative needs (in principle, all), with the minimum of ambiguity, the limit being imposed by his personal concerns and his intellectual capacity and not by the capacity of the medium. As to (c), extensibility may be thought of in terms of 'English for Specific Purposes' modules – which would thus entail the property (independently required in any case) of the lexical and grammatical content being fully explicit, so that the 'fit' of additional modules may be exactly predicted. But extensibility should also be seen in terms of less programmed skill-acquisition towards fully natural English in any major national variety, and this in turn entails that, since nothing should have to be 'unlearned', the lexical and grammatical properties of Nuclear English must be a subset of the properties of natural English (presumably of the 'common core', in the sense of Quirk *et al.* 1972, 1.15).

Both (b) and (c) are obviously vital in their own right. But they are vital also in anticipating misunderstandings about the nature and role of Nuclear English.

Culture-free as calculus, with no literary, aesthetic, or emotional aspirations, Nuclear English is correspondingly more free than the 'national Englishes' of any suspicion that it smacks of linguistic imperialism or even (since native speakers of English would also have to be trained to use it) that it puts some countries at an advantage over others in international communication. Since it is not (but is merely related to) a natural language, it would not be in competition for educational resources with foreign languages proper but rather with that other fundamental interdisciplinary subject, mathematics. Nor, by the same token, could its teachers be accused of wasting resources (as sometimes happens, distressingly, with foreign languages and literatures) on an elitist disciplinary ornament for the few. The relations of Nuclear English are less with the ivory tower than the public convenience.

Equally, however, (b) and (c) make clear that Nuclear English can carry no such stigma as that frequently perceived (however unjustly) in relation to basilect forms of English or the pidgins of tropical seaports. It is not a matter of offering a second-class language to the masses of the twenty-first century where the élite of the nineteenth and twentieth were privileged to have English in all its storied splendour, metaphysicals and all. The emblematic consumers of Nuclear English should not be seen as Indonesian children in a village school room, but as Italian and Japanese company directors engaged in negotiating an agreement.

Reluctantly ignoring issues in the lexicon,[8] let me ponder a little on seeking appropriate nuclei in grammar. It might, for example, be decided that the English tag question (so often in the English of Wales and of Southeast Asia replaced by the invariant *isn't it?* or *is it?*) was disproportionately burdensome, with its requirement of reversed polarity, supply of tensed operator and congruent subject:

> I'm late, *aren't I?/ am I not?*
> She used to work here, *didn't she?*
> They oughtn't to go there, *ought they?*

For all of the italicized pieces, whose function as a response promotor is arguably worth retaining, we could achieve the same objective with *isn't that right?* or *is that so?*, in full English a perfectly acceptable expression though of course a minority one (except as shortened to *right?* in American English).

Or again, there is arguably no need for non-restrictive relative

[8]But see G. Stein, 'Nuclear English: Reflections on the Structure of its Vocabulary', *Poetica* 10 (Tokyo, 1979).

clauses, many of which are in any case semantically inexplicit:

> I chatted with the captain, who was later reprimanded
> I expressed my sympathy to the captain, who had been
> reprimanded

If these mean, respectively,

> I spoke to the captain and *as a result* he was (later) reprimanded
> I expressed my sympathy to the captain *because* he had been
> reprimanded

it would do no harm to say so and at the same time rid us of structures that could be misunderstood (especially in writing) as restrictive clauses. Nor need we retain in Nuclear English the option to construct noun clauses or restrictive relative clauses with 'zero' particle (*He was afraid she was hurt, The man she loves*), and with non-restrictive clauses gone we could generalize *that* as the single invariant particle for relative and noun clauses.

A further example: we need non-finite constructions with certain verbs like *cause* which will almost certainly (unlike perhaps *condescend* and *assist*) remain in the nuclear lexicon: *He caused the experiment to fail*. But we could exclude this construction where it was merely optional for a *that*-clause and hence banish the multiply ambiguous *They expected a doctor to examine John* (the more readily so if, in addition, the lexicon admitted *expect* in only one of the conventional senses).

In none of these instances, it will be noticed, does the 'solution' lie in going beyond the rules of ordinary acceptable English. But – equally noteworthy – for none of the instances has the proposed solution any bearing at all upon frequency of occurrence in ordinary English. If anything (as we shall see below with modal auxiliaries), the most frequent items are those that are most to be excluded from Nuclear English since they are the most polysemous. Rather, the solution must lie in a principled mediation between (a) the grammatical structure of ordinary English and (b) a language-neutral assessment of communicative needs. The order here is vital: the starting point must be (a), not (b). If we adopted the converse, we might for example seek a number system going beyond the existing two terms ('singular' and 'plural') to include a third ('dual') in view of the large number of items in human experience that go in twos (eyes, thumbs, feet, parents etc.). An additional inflection (parent *sg,* parenten *dual*, parents *pl*) would enable us to avoid the ambiguity that is common in sentences like:

The permission of parents is required

(Does each child need to get permission from both parents or will the permission of only one be sufficient?) Needless to say, such a proposal would infringe one of the basic properties of Nuclear English (that it should contain nothing that had to be 'unlearned' by the user who proceeded to any extension beyond it) and would therefore be rejected.

The starting point must therefore remain firmly in the grammar of ordinary English, and the major systems (like countability, transitivity, gender, tense) will be retained along with their ordinary exponents, their use defined explicitly in terms of relevant communicative needs. By 'major systems' would be understood those affecting more than one word-class and having reverberations on other systems – as in the case of the count/non-count distinction which is reflected both in the determiner system and in verb inflection.

Much research and experiment will be necessary to find out the extent to which these principles can be translated into a blueprint for prescribing the grammar of Nuclear English. Unquestionably, there will be many problems in identifying for omission those minor systems for which alternative expression can be found within major ones. Thus (in terms of Quirk *et al.* 1972) 'complex transitive' and 'ditransitive' structures might reasonably be excised from the transitivity system. We glimpsed a possible treatment of complex transitives in the *expect* example above. Ditransitives are on the face of it even easier to handle – through replacement by the corresponding prepositional alternative:

We offered the girl a drink → We offered a drink *to the girl*

But there is the problem of certain verbs for which there is no prepositional alternative (cf. *He charged her a high rent*) and of verbs on the other hand which have alternative prepositional complementation (cf. *serve X to Y = serve Y with X*). It is of course likely that verbs with such lexical compression would be replaced by nuclear periphrases (*He caused her to pay a high rent, He said that it was necessary that she pay . . .*), but to the extent that such verbs are retained in the lexicon on purely lexicological grounds, they present interesting difficulties as to grammatical treatment.

More miscellanea of this kind could be easily supplied, but I shall confine my attention to the problems posed by the modals, an area of notorious difficulty in English and other languages, and liable to cause difficulty in communication even between native speakers. I shall begin with a reminder of the complexities, and in the course of what follows I shall attempt to project what must be conveyed in Nuclear English.

Take one of those doom-laden stellar conjunctions beloved of Arthur Hailey. We're in an electric storm over Indiana on a flight from New York (hereafter designated – quite fictitiously, needless to say – Able Baker 123). In the bad and intermittent radio reception, our pilot hears a ground control voice:

> Able Baker 123 may land at O'Hare in five minutes

Now, it is easy for the philosopher or linguist in his study to see that this is ambiguous. But for the ordinary speaker in discourse, including the ordinary pilot on the flight deck, speech contains no ambiguities: we tune in to the meaning that happens to be uppermost in our expectations. If the pilot thinks he is merely eavesdropping on a message about his aircraft to someone else, he will at once interpret it as:

> Able Baker 123 will possibly land at O'Hare in five minutes

– an expression of opinion which he will check against the probabilities suggested by other factors, including his instruments. If on the other hand he takes it to be a message addressed to himself, he will just as instantaneously interpret it as:

> Able Baker 123 is permitted to land at O'Hare in five minutes

– a very different matter indeed. Either way, radio conditions may make it difficult to check or correct the interpretation.

If the radioed sentence used *can* and referred to an airfield not on his flight plan (say, Fort Wayne, Indiana), further possibilities occur, again without warning the hearer of their existence:

> Able Baker 123 can land at Fort Wayne

This could still mean 'is permitted to land', but it might equally mean 'has the capability of landing' (i.e. can adopt the right approach angle or has the appropriate landing speed for Fort Wayne; or Fort

Wayne has a sufficiently long runway for a 747, or whatever). Then again, interpreted as a message between two controllers, the sentence could be interpreted as:

> It is conceivable that we could divert Able Baker 123 to Fort Wayne

Introduce a past marking and new ambiguities appear:

> Able Baker 123 could have landed at Fort Wayne

(= either 'had the capability of landing . . . but didn't'; or 'had the possibility . . . but didn't'; or 'had permission to land . . . but didn't'; or even 'It is possible that 123 did in fact land'.)

Withdrawing from air travel melodrama, we find analogous ambiguities with other modal expressions:

> They ought to be here

can mean 'There was a requirement that they be here'; or 'I expect that they are here'; or 'I expected that they were here, but they're not'.

> John WILL fail his exams!

can mean 'I confidently predict that he will'; or 'John persists in failing'; or even 'I insist on his failing'.

> John must stay at home on Wednesdays

can mean 'John is obliged to stay at home' or 'It seems certain that John stays at home'.

> John is supposed to be asleep

can mean 'There is a requirement on John to be asleep'; or 'There is a requirement on us to believe that John is asleep'; or 'People suppose that John is asleep'.

Not suprisingly, as every EFL teacher knows, errors among foreign learners are legion and apparently ineradicable.[9] Even non-

---

[9]They must not of course be exaggerated. In the first place, there are grossly overloaded modality systems in other languages beside English, and the same analogies and 'metaphors' are very generally involved. Secondly, pragmatic factors (including common sense) often preclude misunderstanding: *May I go?* is unlikely to be epistemic since a person does not ask other people about what in the nature of things

natives in post as university professors of English (let alone professionals in other disciplines, whatever their fluency) make errors like the following; indeed I have taken them from such sources:

You could like to forward the book to me	(for *might*)
For this reason he would not write it	(for *would not be writing*)
The study should be of great value	(for *would*)
The conductor arrived and the concert should start	(for *was due to*)
After many attempts, he could succeed	(for *was able to*)
The students had better write clearly	(for *should*)
He tells me that he must write it last year	(for *had to*)

There are additional difficulties lurking in the relation between assertive and non-assertive modality. Thus, although with some modals the correspondence is straightforward (*He can drive a car: He can't . . ./ If he can . . ./ Can he . . . ?*), with others it is not, and quite experienced non-natives are apt to slip into expressions like:

He must not complete his thesis before January
He may not answer every question

where 'need not, is permitted not to' happens to be meant in both cases. And among the further difficulties, there are those arising from differences in discourse orientation: the contrasting expectations involved between for example *He may go* (which will probably be deontic but may be epistemic) and *I may go* (which will almost certainly be epistemic but may be deontic). (Cf. Palmer, 1974: 100ff.)

The problems inherent in modality have of course long been the subject of discussion. In that pioneer study of linguistic engineering, the *Essay Towards a Real Character* of 1668, John Wilkins distinguished 'primary' and 'secondary modes', the latter being concerned in 'modal propositions' where 'the Matter in discourse . . . is concerned not *simply by itself*, but *gradually in its causes*' (316). These modal propositions he sees as involving either contingency or necessity, each being itself bipartite. So far as con-

---

he must know better than anyone else. Thirdly, in many instances modal properties effectively merge, however theoretically distinct they may be: *He can leave immediately* cannot normally involve possibility without simultaneously involving permission.

tingency is concerned, either the speaker expresses 'only the *Possibility*' of something (which is dependent 'upon the power of its cause'), or 'his own *Liberty* to it'(when there is 'a freedom from all Obstacles either within or without'). With *necessity*, says Wilkins, 'the speaker expresseth the resolution of his own will' or '*some external obligation*, whether *Natural* or *Moral*'. As we could expect from this, when Wilkins comes subsequently to propose his 'real characters', he offers distinct symbols for each of these modal values (391).

It seems clear that Nuclear English cannot afford to do less. Whether we need more distinctions is quite another question. It will be noticed that Wilkins anticipates modern philosophers and linguists in his insistence on awareness of the speaker's involvement, but I am doubtful whether we need to follow more recent scholars in recognizing – at any rate explicitly – a three-tier modality in every sentence (designated neustic, tropic, and phrastic in Hare, 1970). But in view of the unfortunate overlaps demonstrable in the ordinary English use of modals, it seems clear that such factors bearing upon propositional content as the speaker's commitment, the factuality, and the constraint upon the agent need to be given formal expression.

Within speaker's commitment, we need further to bear in mind the relevant contrasts arising as between his knowledge, his belief, his desire and his mere declaration. Factuality involves the range from certainty through probability to possibility and improbability. With constraints upon the agent, it is important to distinguish on the one hand between those that are internal to the agent (whether relating to his ability or to his volition) and those that are external to him (whether compulsion or absolute *necessity* on the one hand, or social or moral *duty* on the other).

These parameters enjoin the recognition of three theoretically quite distinct types of modality. We have *epistemic* modality expressing the degree of speaker's knowledge (e.g. *He may go* = 'I think it possible that he will'); *deontic* or 'root' modality expressing constraint, whether imposed by the speaker (as in imperatives) or by some other agency (such as the law); and *potential* modality, concerned with the agent's volition or ability. A fourth modality, *alethic* (cf. Lyons 1977), can be disregarded in ordinary linguistic communication, concerned as it is with purely logical necessity ('Since he is unmarried, he must be a bachelor').

The question now arises as to how these modalities and their partially overlapping concerns with speaker, agent, and external world might best be expressed in Nuclear English. We might consider three possibilities.

(a) We could try to separate off those that are in some sense most 'important'[10] and disregard the rest. This seems in effect to be what happens in pidgin languages such as Neo-Melanesian, but among its objectionable aspects would be the failure thereby to meet the requirement that Nuclear English must provide full communicative adequacy.

(b) We could retain the ordinary range of English modals but restrict their use to avoid overlap. Thus *may* might be restricted to epistemic use ('be possible') and excluded from deontic use ('be permitted'). This proposal has several disadvantages. It would tend not to oblige the speaker to analyse the precise intention of his message, and it would be very difficult for the speaker with a partial or good knowledge of 'full' English to avoid making 'mistakes' and forming just such ambiguous sentences as were illustrated earlier.

(c) We could retain the full range of modalities but restrict their expression to carefully prescribed and maximally explicit paraphrases,[11] banning the use of the normal modal auxiliaries altogether.

This is a sharply radical proposal but it is of course in line with the theory of Nuclear English as envisaged in this paper. In repudiating the claims of 'frequency in occurrence', we would achieve the objective of avoiding the ultimately far greater disdavantages of extreme polysemy. In requiring paraphrase, we would be insisting on a speaker's clarifying his own intention in advance, while yet expressing himself without departure from fully acceptable forms of ordinary English. Indeed, paraphrases of the kind 'It is possible that this is not true', 'It is not possible that this is true' present the means not only of separating modality from proposition but of stipulating

[10]In this connection, it would be worth exmining the implications of current work by Gordon Wells of Bristol on the order and rate of acquiring modal expression in children and on the types and distribution of modal values expressed in parent-child interaction.

[11]In the present programmatic outline, the specific properties of the optimal paraphrases must be ignored. Among the formidable topics for study, however, is the nature of deontic passives like 'is obliged', 'is permitted' and the question of specifying agency.

such features as the scope of negation, frequently obscured in ordinary language. In all of which, we achieve a mode of expression reflecting distinctions that have been the subject of considerable discussion in the 'higher sentence' debate of current linguistics (cf. Ross 1969, Anderson 1971, Erdmann 1977). Indeed, it could even be argued (cf. Lightfoot 1974) that our proposal would amount to 'restoring' predications that have been submerged in the course of linguistic history.

It will be seen that Nuclear English is conceived as having great power but also as exercising drastic constraints. Not only is the language to be learned by the non-native carefully and explicitly restricted: so equally must the language of the native speaker be constrained to a precisely corresponding extent when he is using Nuclear English as an international medium. A tall order? Yes, but surely more than a mere pipe dream if we consider the continuous thought that has been given to these issues from Francis Bacon onwards – and if we take seriously the issue of international needs.

The word *international* was coined nearly 200 years ago by a man whose mortal remains, clothed and seated, are on prominent display at my place of work, University College London. Jeremy Bentham's utilitarianism explicitly and emphatically embraced questions of linguistic engineering. He was impressed by Francis Bacon's observation that learning suffers 'distemper' through the fact that words effectively mask and obscure the 'weight of matter' that should be at the centre of our attention (*Advancement of Learning*, 1605). Bentham based his concern for the clarification of linguistic expression on the great tradition that extended from Bacon, through Comenius, Mersenne, Wilkins, Leibniz, Berkeley, to Horne Tooke in his own day. Indeed he strove (vainly, as it turned out) to have appointed as the first Professor of English in my College the polyglot John Bowring who was keen on the notion of establishing a universal language.

This 'great tradition' was seriously disrupted by the advent of comparative philology in the early nineteenth century, and the subsequent development of phonetics – in part supportive of it, in part directed in the opposite direction: the examination of the material actually heard (the 'substance features') in living languages. This in turn gave a different emphasis in language teaching (towards speech fluency, measured especially in terms of phonetic accuracy), while the embracing by the universities of these twin branches of inquiry, phonology and comparative philology, as the dominant foci of intellectual excitement, had the effect of pushing philosophical linguistics and universalism back from the footlights. Though never entirely forgotten by academic philosophers, it was only a minority of linguists who persisted with their interest, and those have been largely on the periphery of the academic establishment. One thinks of Ogden, Korzybski, Hayakawa, and the pages of *ETC*, etc.

With our discovery of J. L. Austin – some years after his death – and with a greater catholicity, eclecticism, and perhaps pragmatism in linguistic theory than we have known for nearly half a century, I feel that this is the time for serious re-engagement with the issues that occupied Wilkins and his successors.

References

Anderson, J. 1971: 'Some Proposals Concerning the Modal Verbs in English', in *Edinburgh Studies in English and Scots* (ed. A.J. Aitken *et al.*). London: Longman.

Erdmann, P. 1977: 'On Deriving Deontic Modals'. *Linguistics* **192**.

Fishman, J. et al. 1968: *Language Problems in Developing Nations*. New York: Wiley.

Hare, R.M. 1970: 'Meaning and Speech Acts'. *Philosophical Review* **79**.

Kachru, B. 1976: 'Indian English: A Sociolinguistic Profile of a Transplanted Language', in *Studies in Language Learning* **1** (Urbana: University of Illinois Press).

Lightfoot, D.W. 1974: 'The Diachronic Analysis of English Modals', in *Historical Linguistics* **1** (ed. J.M. Anderson and C. Jones). Amsterdam: North-Holland.

Lyons, J. 1977: *Semantics*. Cambridge: Cambridge University Press.

Palmer, F.R. 1974: *The English Verb*. London: Longman.

Quirk, R. 1972: *The English Language and Images of Matter*. London: Oxford University Press.

—1978: 'Aspects of English as an International Language'. *Sproglaereren* **9**.

Quirk, R., Greenbaum, S., Leech, G. and Svartvik, J. 1972: *A Grammar of Contemporary English*. London: Longman.

Ross, J.R. 1969: 'Auxiliaries as Main Verbs, in *Studies in Philosophical Linguistics* **1** (ed. W. Todd). Evanston, Illinois: Northwestern University Press.

Strevens, P. 1977: *New Orientations in the Teaching of English*. Oxford: Oxford University Press.

4 Language and Nationhood

'I do not recollect that anyone has drawn a significant parallel between Aristophanes and Chaucer' (MacQueen 1971). With this ironic concluding sentence of a paper on early Scottish literature, Professor John MacQueen is making a contrast with David Lindsay, in whose *Satire of the Three Estates* he does indeed see parallels with Aristophanes.

Although I shall not dwell on Scottish linguistic, literary and national issues, Scotland is of course an appropriate starting point – as is Sir David Lindsay. He was writing in a period long before the Act of Union, at a time when political independence matched a general cultural integrity that enabled nationhood to be taken for granted.

This cultural integrity embraced a literature that was independent of – though drawing confidently upon – classical, medieval, and contemporary materials, not least English materials such as the work of Chaucer. The confidence is what I would like to stress: the literature could assert its wholeness and dignity without either apologizing for any imitation of foreign material on the one hand or stridently asserting its specific Scottishness on the other. Interesting confirmation of this self-confidence appears in the medium by which the literature was transmitted: a language distinct in lexicon, grammar and phonology from the language of London, if anything in advance of London English so far as standardization is concerned (for example, in orthography). And the confidence is underlined by the way Scots often referred to their language – with realistic pragmatism – as 'Inglis'). The recognition of its distinctiveness, yet at the same time of its roots in Anglo-Saxon, is interestingly illustrated by the fact that in the seventeenth century we find William L'Isle choos-

Note: An earlier form of this chapter first appeared in *The Crown and the Thistle*, edited by Colin MacLean (1979).

ing to read a translation of Virgil in Scots because this language was closer to the 'Saxon' than was the standard English of London (Simon 1961). At the same time, the fact that Scotsmen could call their tongue 'Inglis', plainly perceiving its close relation to what was spoken south of the border, by no means precluded an equally clear recognition that it was 'the language of Scottis natioun'. Thus Gavin Douglas, for instance (cf. Bawcutt 1976).

If sociolinguists are right in putting awareness of cultural greatness as one of the three conditions for mature nationhood (cf. Fishman 1971), then the raison d'être of the quotation with which I began is itself not without interest. Professor MacQueen was stating 'The Case for Early Scottish Literature', not because the Scottish literary tradition is 'quite separate from that of the English' but because it is indeed 'a Great Tradition' (by the highest – and least parochial – standards: hence the appeal to Aristophanes) and because the study of this literature has been neglected. The implication is clearly that in recent centuries there has been a decline not perhaps so much in the consciousness of Scottish nationhood as in the confidence with which it could be asserted.

I shall not forget that I am speaking in Scotland (nor yet that I travelled here from England), but for the moment let me move forward in time and further in space. On 4 July 1974 the late Jomo Kenyatta proclaimed, with all the blunt resolve that we associate with him, that Swahili was to be the national language of Kenya, from that very day onwards. On the face of it, and from the viewpoint of internal administration (let alone education, trade, external affairs, and several other factors), this was perhaps a surprising decision. English was (and is) the chief medium in all these matters and its use was rapidly increasing (as apparently it still is). Moreover, Swahili is not one of the language in Kenya with a major following by way of native speakers – and especially not in the capital, Nairobi. If this had been a criterion, Kikuyu would have been a much more obvious choice. But this would have been dangerously divisive, given the racial balance of power in Kenya.[1] Yet having divined that the time had come when Kenya's sense of nationhood had to be underwritten, not merely by national flag, anthem,

---

[1] Not that Swahili is without its dangers. Writing only three or four years before Kenyatta's declaration, Whiteley (1971) claimed that 'precedence for Swahili would lead to strong reactions from the powerful groups on either side of the Rift Valley.' In any event, and for whatever reason, Kenyatta's edict was revoked in May 1979.

airline and such predictable trappings of independence, but also by the more pervasive symbol of a national language, Kenyatta was equally convinced – as Lyndon Harries has argued (1976) – that it had to be an African language. So the choice fell upon Swahili.

Doubtless the move was triggered off by what had happened in neighbouring Tanzania, though there the solution had been simpler. Swahili has a very considerable currency in Tanzania, not least in the capital, Dar-es-Salaam, where the majority of the population speak it as their mother tongue. In consequence, standardization on the basis of educated speech in the capital can be seen as rather straightforward. The position in Kenya is very different. The population of Nairobi has relatively little access to native models of Swahili, educated or otherwise, and they must look for these to the Islamic coastal regions far from the capital.

The problem of creating a sense of state-nationhood is of course particularly severe in Africa. To take only that vast and complex area south of the Sahara, there are some forty-two different 'countries' each trying to make itself a nation: but these countries comprise a total population of about 250 million people speaking well over 700 entirely different languages. We scarcely need to remind ourselves that many of the newly independent countries are functioning with frontiers that have emerged less from the natural cut-and-thrust of the indigenous peoples than from the territorial division made in the European cabinet offices of the former colonial powers. Nonetheless, the situation in Kenya that I have outlined has uncomfortable parallels nearer home. One thinks of Nynorsk – no less the result of nationalist aspiration and political decision, and equally lacking a natural currency in the capital, Oslo. One thinks of Irish, proclaimed from English-speaking Dublin as the national language of Ireland.[2]

Nor do the parallels end with opting for a national language without firm roots in the national capital. In each of these cases, we see a political establishment deliberately seeking to downgrade a language associated with an earlier foreign domination: English in two instances, Swedish and Danish (Bokmål) in the third. At the same time – in a perfectly understandable reaction – there is the aim to put in its place a language with unassailable claims to being

---

[2]Even the equably multilingual Switzerland is not without its problems in this respect. The numerically preponderant language, German, has its standard not in Zürich but in High German, beyond the Swiss frontier.

indigenous, however deficient in widespread currency.[3]

I have deliberately described the Kenyan situation in terms of an implied but unspecified norm, and the extent to which this may not have been noticed is a measure of how deeply ingrained our expectation of this norm has become – as though it is self-evident, inevitable, and above all perfectly natural. Since I want eventually to call this norm into question, let me at this stage spell it out.

The concept of nationhood clearly rests upon unity of interest, and there are many factors which bring this about. An obvious one is geographical integrity. It is difficult to preserve nationhood with geographical division – and almost impossible to create, as Pakistan found. But geographical definition needs endorsement in community of race (a much vaguer and more variable concept than we tend to think, despite all the agonizing lessons in *Rassenkunde* we have been taught by recent history), and if possible also in religion, history, economic necessity, tradition, culture: 'way of life', let us lamely say. And of course I have still not mentioned the element with which I am chiefly concerned: language.[4] We have come to take it as axiomatic that the norm of national unity is linguistic unity: one nation, one language, with its standards determined by and emanating from the nation's capital – the seat of political authority being the seat of linguistic authority, as well as authority in other respects (taste in architecture, literature, couture). In the view of some, of course, nation is actually defined in terms of language: a language community constitutes a nation. The eighteenth-century philosopher, von Herder, is among the many who have contributed to the virtually orthodox view that a nation without its own language is a contradiction in terms (Fishman 1973). This is confirmed by the names of nations and languages which many would hold to be both the norm and the ideal: the language of Italy is Italian, of Finland Finnish, of Hungary Hungarian, of Poland Polish, of Japan Japanese.

Now of course there are counter-examples. Many nation-states speak the same language as others. We have Arabic in such very

[3]Indigenous, ethnic authenticity is of course the obvious criterion where tribal rivalries permit a simple selection. On this basis, nineteenth-century nationalism saw the 'emergence' of Slovak, Ukrainian, Rumanian, Estonian, Finnish and several other 'national languages' which we now take for granted.

[4]To judge from Beloded (1977), this seems to be the chief criterion for identifying what are referred to as the many 'nations' of the USSR, 'a multinational unity of peoples', where it is claimed that 'no national language can be belittled.'

different independent countries as Egypt and Iraq; Spanish in Cuba as well as Argentina: English in Britain as well as the United States. On the other hand, there are nation-states with more than one language spoken within their frontiers. In Switzerland we have German, French, Italian and Romansch; in Singapore, Malay, Chinese, Tamil and English. Indeed some of the largest member countries of the United Nations are in this position: the Soviet Union with Russian, Ukrainian, Lithuanian, Georgian, Armenian, and scores of others (Beloded 1977); India with a still greater linguistic profusion. Nor are the UK and USA as linguistically simplex and monolithic as the majority like to think.

But here we must pause to acknowledge (if not to disentangle) a serious problem of terminology. Both 'lânguage' and 'nation', despite their formal discreteness as words, are notoriously slippery in meaning. And like the slippery creatures of which Othello speaks with such distaste, they 'knot and gender' to spawn still slipperier creatures called 'national languages'. *Nation* (despairingly omitted from many encyclopedias) can refer to a political entity – as in the American constitution; to the individuals 'belonging' to that entity (as in expressions like 'The nation was united as they faced the enemy'); and to groups evincing ethnic or cultural solidarity (usually involving the adjectival form, as in expressions like 'national minorities'). And such national groups may be subordinate within political entities; or they may be superordinate to them, as when we talk of African national consciousness or national confederations of Arab states. I need scarcely say that these ambiguities are far from unknown in our own islands, not least in these devolutionary days.

Filling out a customs form at Kennedy Airport, I unhesitatingly enter 'British' where I am told to state my nationality. But British nationals rarely talk about the 'British nation', and would have difficulty in defining it if they were challenged. While 'nation' is applied freely enough to Scotland and Wales and Ireland, the idea of England as a nation is ironically strange. And it would not occur to us to apply the word to Kent.

Now, since 'nation' (via 'nationalism') is so caught up in ideology, the variability and ambiguity may not surprise us. But surely 'language' is straightforward: everyone can hear immediately when a different language is spoken. Not so, I fear. We certainly detect linguistic differences very readily, even from person to person, village to village. Sometimes they are so great that we can't understand what is being said – when we hear Japanese being spoken, for instance. But that is not what makes Japanese a different language from English. Danish and Swedish are different languages but they are mutually intelligible. Speakers of Urdu and Hindi can understand each other as easily as Yorkshire men are understood in Sussex; so too, speakers of Polish and Slovak. People seek to have their form of speech dignified by the name of 'language' when they need thus to assert this form of self-respect. And this of course is why language interacts with nationalist ideology. It has long been – and remains – an insistent rallying point in nationalist movements,[5] and just as extremes of nationalist ideology engage with the theory (and sometimes with the drastic practice) of racial purity, so do the protagonists of national languages tend to involve themselves with questions of linguistic purity. Even the pragmatic English have flirted with the idea from time to time (cf. Simon 1961), and several languages – German is a classic example – have been drastically refurbished on this basis (cf. Kloss 1952, Polenz 1967).[6] But even in the least doctrinaire thinking, language is often taken to be the most important of the nation-endorsing factors that I have mentioned, and on the face of it even the most rational of them. In a sense, the most palpable. Geographical entities shade into one another except where there are major mountain or water barriers. Racial distinctions are often imperceptible and in any case racial mixture is not

---

[5]Both in movements within a polity (e.g. Breton in France) and in movements on a pan-nationalist scale, embracing distinct polities: thus 'An Arab is a person whose mother tongue is Arabic . . . and who believes in being a member of the Arab nation' (from the Constitution of the Ba'athist Party, quoted in Fishman 1973).

[6]Johann Gottlieb Fichte was an early protagonist of the moves to 'purge' German of 'foreign impurities' (especially French), whereby the language could become superior *per se* and a fitter vehicle by which to express German nationhood. The French have been concerned with linguistic purity (especially directed against Anglicisms) for over a century, and purity has been extolled as a criterion in connection with Finnish, Turkish, Urdu, Hindi and Irish, among many other examples (Fishman 1973). Occasional attacks on Americanisms in Britain (and on 'Briticisms' in the United States) are faint echoes of the same sociolinguistic thunder. Although the ideology of linguistic nationalism was never strong or sustained in Britain, the recent anti-Franglais law in France should remind us that such ideology is by no means relegated to a primitive past. The deliberate Islamic injections into 'High Urdu', the struggle in Greece to promote the classically-orientated Katharevousa, and the accentuation of India's language problems by 'purifying' Hindi on a Sanskrit basis stand as current witnesses. Several observers have pointed to the irony of emergent nationhood eagerly getting rid of foreign blood and foreign words while just as eagerly (often promiscuously) absorbing foreign ideas – arguably far more corrosive of national uniqueness.

merely easy but normal. Religious differences are not usually obvious – though Northern Ireland apparently provides one of the many exceptions to this. But even the most superficial contact between people lays starkly bare any linguistic differences – not merely between peoples and social groups but within social groups.

There are thus sound enough grounds for the nation-language norm, and of course plenty of canonical exempla of this norm in operation. France and Portugal are long-standing instances, and the 'emergent' nations of more recent European history are very generally on this model: Germany, Rumania, Finland, Albania, to name but an obvious few. As Haugen (1966) puts it, 'Nation and language have become inextricably intertwined. Every self-respecting nation has to have a language. Not just a medium of communication, a "vernacular" or a "dialect", but a fully developed language. Anything less marks it as underdeveloped.' In this lies the tendency to proliferation that we find with newly recognised 'languages' as with newly established 'nations' – newly 'invented' nations, as some – perhaps unkindly – put it (cf. Gellner 1964).

The goal of a single national language may be pursued on purely rational grounds, even where the language selected is far from being the one spoken natively by the majority of citizens. There are numerous examples round the world of a former colonial language becoming accepted as the national language simply for the pragmatic reason that it is there, already in use for administration, education and trade. This can occur even in territories where the language concerned has virtually no native currency: the present moves to ratify the adoption of English as the sole national language of Nigeria are a case in point. Elsewhere we see deliberate 'linguistic engineering' at work to adapt indigenous tongues to forge a standard language of national unity. Thus we have Serbo-Croatian in Yugoslavia and the modernization of Hebrew in Israel.

There is a particularly striking example in Indonesia. During Dutch rule in the East Indies, the colonial language was of course general in administration and in much of the education system. But already in the early years of the present century, the independence movement had opted for Malay as the language in which to rouse support and to create a feeling of unity (Alisjahbana 1974). Dutch would not do, since – for one thing – insufficient people knew it for propaganda to be effective. Yet the choice of Malay is not on the face of it obvious. It was certainly not dominant numerically

– outnumbered by Javanese, for example, in a ratio of about three to one. But throughout the vast archipelago (and indeed more widely in South-East Asia), Malay had acquired a status comparable to that of English on the larger world scale: it was the lingua franca carried by travellers and traders, and thus widely understood, if remaining the mother tongue of only a minority. It was thus a natural and rational choice for the independence movement to use throughout the area and subsequently to decide upon as the language of the future independent nation. In 1928 an onomastic decision was taken with political significance: the movement would henceforth refer to Malay as 'Indonesian' (*Bahasa Indonesia*). Tongues of men and tingling symbols. A language by another name sounds not so sweet. But of course, as with the transformation in Norway of Landsmål to Nynorsk, more came to be involved than just nomenclature.

With the invasion of 1942, vigorous steps were at once taken to replace Dutch by Japanese in all respects and at all levels. But not even the Japanese could achieve overnight what the Dutch had attempted for more than three centuries, and so the new masters adroitly switched their interest to Indonesian, capitalising on the work of the anti-Dutch independence movement. Before the end of 1942, they had set up a commission (including such men as Achmed Sukarno, later to become the first President of independent Indonesia) to standardize and modernize the language. At the same time they adopted Indonesian for administrative purposes and did the independence movement's work for it by spreading the use of this language throughout the entire territory.

It is difficult of course for an outsider to gauge the extent to which Bahasa Indonesia has contributed to moulding Indonesian nationhood. But despite the fact that it is effectively the mother tongue of little more than ten per cent of the population (which numbers almost 130 million), there can be no doubt about its success as a medium of communication, administration and education. Meanwhile, the work of modernizing and improving the language has continued; and by 1970 no less than one quarter of a million words had been coined since 1942.[7]

And it is not only new nations that feel, from time to time, the need to modernize, reorientate or even replace their national

---

[7]The creation of a language of national unity in the Philippines was on similar lines: Pilipino is a development of Tagalog, native to only a fifth of the population.

language. In the century and a quarter of its 'post-Perry' era, Japan has given serious thought to abandoning Japanese and adopting in its place a national language (English and French have been the chief candidates) by which the country could more rapidly attain scientific and industrial development (Miller 1977). Whether this could have been practicable, given the size of the Japanese population (even when the question was last mooted with particular keenness, 1946, the population was over seventy-three million), recent economic history has certainly shown that rapid development needed no such linguistic revolution.

A kind of linguistic revolution has however been felt necessary in China, though of course of a much less radical nature, following the establishment nearly 30 years ago of the People's Republic. The need for rapid economic development called for a close look at internal communication and the definition of the most appropriate standard for a national language which, however unitary in its written (basically ideographic) form, is notoriously diverse in speech. The difference between some 'dialects' of Chinese is as great as that between numerous European 'languages'. The census of 1953 showed that 70 per cent of the country's population (then given as about 600 million) spoke some Northern form of Chinese – in effect a form of what had been called Mandarin, the language of the old imperial Court in Peking. This entirely unsurprising result was however put to good use. It provided a democratic (rather than a mandarin) basis for defining a new standard based upon the Chinese of Peking and called *p'u-t'ung-hua* – 'common speech', or PTH for short. A conference on standardization in 1955 characterized PTH 'as a speech form based phonologically on the dialect of Peking, grammatically on the structure of the North Chinese dialect group, and lexically and stylistically on the works of certain representative modern Chinese writers' (Barnes 1974). Subsequently, and again unsurprisingly, Mao Tse-tung was specified as one of the modern writers whose Chinese could be taken as a model. Doubtless of more substance is the fact that defining PTH in terms of a new standard provides a basis on which rapid recognition can be given to the new terms that modern science and industrialization require. At the same time the voice of Peking Radio, near enough to local Peking speech to be democratically justified, while distinct enough to raise it beyond identification with a specific region, is a satisfactory compromise in the pursuit of a suitable language through which national unity can be forged (an *Ausbau* language: cf. Kloss 1952).

Although I have been using the word 'democratic', it will not have gone unnoticed that some of the most noteworthy steps in the selecting and developing of a national language have been taken in political circumstances that are something less than 'democratic' in the sense normally given this word in our own culture-in Kenyatta's Kenya, for example, and in Indonesia under the Japanese and later under Sukarno. Other instances could be given of where radical proposals concerning language in relation to nationhood have a better chance of succeeding (perhaps even of being conceived in the first place) under autocratic rule. Perhaps the story of Turkish in the Atatürk period 1923–38 is the best known – and justly so (cf. Rubin and Jernudd 1971, Fishman 1974).

The search for national identity through national language in liberal democratic societies has had its victories, but their number has been in inverse proportion to their degree of radicalism. Certainly the dogged efforts to replace well established languages in Norway and Ireland have met with only modest success – and even these were at least conceived in circumstances apprehended as the autocracy of foreign oppression and were the response of nationalist feeling to the languages of dominant neighbours.

In Ireland, as in Indonesia, plans were going ahead long before independence so that free nationhood – when it should emerge – could be enshrined in a national language appropriately distinct from the language of a regime that had been dominant for hundreds of years. But there the similarity largely ends. On the one hand, Irish patriots could call upon a rich literary, artistic and religious heritage, strongly associated with a Celtic language having continuous records for over a millennium. There was thus a ready-made language of mature nationhood waiting in the wings (and indeed it was already being fostered by the British, twenty years before independence). On the other hand, English had achieved a degree of currency in Ireland incomparably greater than had Dutch in the East Indies. The restitution of Irish was bound therefore to meet formidable opposition, and the advent of broadcasting almost simultaneously with independence meant not merely a continuity of exposure to English but a drastic extension of it, given the wider variety of programmes transmitted from London than from Dublin – in the 1920s as in the 1970s. Perhaps above all, there was the disincentive to use Irish arising from the fact that English was (and remains) the language of Dublin; I have already (in relation to Nairobi and Oslo) drawn attention to the obvious difficulty of establishing a national language which is other than the language of the national capital.

On top of that again, but directly related to it, has been the problem of standardization. The prestige of Irish as the language of the great medieval literature was secure enough. The prestige of the living Irish (chiefly of the peasantry in the Western provinces – the Gaeltacht) was another matter entirely, in whatever glow of affection and nationalist fervour it was held by patriots. Grammars and dictionaries and teaching materials had to be prepared, orthography had to be revised, new terms had to be adopted or coined, competing forms in the living dialects had to be evaluated.[8]

Not surprisingly in view of all this, the constitutional statement about Irish being 'the national language' and 'first official language' remains more a hope than a fact. A fairly recent statement (1964)[9] reiterates the aim that Irish 'should once again be a normal means of conversation and communication among Irish people', this having been 'the linguistic objective of every government since the foundation of the Sate'. A government paper of Comhairle na Gaeilge in 1972 provided estimates of the rather unimpressive achievement to date: probably less than 5 per cent of ordinary conversation in Ireland is carried on in Irish – 'much higher for a typical Gaeltacht resident and lower for others'. Even the medium-term goal laid down in this paper is modest in terms of usage for a 'national language': 20 per cent of ordinary discourse 'outside the Gaeltacht by the end of the century'. Meantime, in the 1961 census, although Irish had been a compulsory school subject for nearly 40 years, 73 per cent of the population declared itself to be non-Irish speaking. Eamon De Valera once said that he would willingly give up all he knew of English to speak Irish properly (Bromage 1956). He did not, however, and neither has his people.

Now, of course, when we think of Irish literature we think primarily of O'Casey, Beckett, Joyce, Synge, Yeats and their forebears: a long and undoubtedly Great Tradition of writers in English. But not simply the English of England. At their most characteristic,

---

[8]Fishman (1970) documents numerous instances of emergent nations – Finland, Estonia, Turkey, for instance – where language standardization was sought on the basis of the 'unspoiled' peasant's speech.
[9]Cf. Macnamara (1971) and the papers of Comhairle na Gaeilge in Fishman (1974).

these writers use an English that is as Irish as the Dáil (rather precisely so, in fact) and arguably much more Irish than the peat fire. So it is with the voice of Radio Telefís Éireann, heard most frequently in English but unmistakably the English of Ireland, recognizable as such in any part of the English-speaking world (as some sort of ability to imitate it shows clearly enough). Frank public statements on Irish English and its status are still rare, and standardization has proceeded largely without benefit of any official establishment structure corresponding to Comhairle na Gaeilge, but the fact is that the chief national language of the Irish Republic is cultivated Irish English. Irish history, north as well as south, might well have been different if the constitution had designated *this* as 'Irish' and had proceeded from the 1920s to make explicit its standards with the full panoply of dictionary and other insignia of linguistic independence.

This happened, mutatis mutandis, after 1776. The ten young United States had no less reason than Ireland to proclaim their freedom from the linguistic shackles of London. In 1788 a Philological Society was set up in New York with 'the purpose of ascertaining and improving the *American Tongue*'. 'The AMERICAN LANGUAGE,' proclaimed William Thornton in 1793 (and one can almost hear the full capitals in which this was printed), 'will . . . be as distinct as the government.' At about the same time, there appeared Noah Webster's *Dissertations* in which he urged spelling changes, since these would enhance the differences between the English of America and that of Britain – a desideratum, because 'a national language is a band of national union.'[10] It is no surprise, therefore, that in 1800 Webster saw it as 'necessary that we should have Dictionaries' of what he boldly called 'the *American Language*', and he set about it with such vigour and success that his name has become almost synonymous with 'dictionary'. In 1828, we find Fenimore Cooper asserting that 'an entirely different standard for

[10]Linguists have tended to think of spelling as peripheral and trivial, but in the context of endowing a 'national language' with identity and dignity (given the importance of education, literacy and the printed 'face' of the language in independence movements), spelling can assume a considerable role. Examples are the institutionalization of Pidgin in Papua New Guinea as Neo-Melanesian (Quirk 1972) and the difference between Serbian and Croatian as accentuated by Cyrillic and Roman letters; and in the 1840s it was in no small measure the separate spelling introduced by the Austrian authorities that identified Slovak as distinct from Czech (Fishman 1973). Cf. also the development of 'pin-yin' (romanized spelling), in contemporary China.

the language must be established . . . from that which governs so absolutely in England.' And all this, in sharp distinction from what I have said about Irish English, long before anyone outside America could have confidently identified an American from his speech (Quirk 1972).

Now of course much of the talk about linguistic independence reflected the nationalist aspirations of the few, rather than either linguistic fact or the implicit cultural allegiance of the many. Just as some of the pressure to develop Irish was aimed at diminishing the pull of fashions in language and culture across the sea; just as Canadians find it difficult to develop a distinctive identity because of the powerful American magnet south of the 49th parallel; just indeed as Professor MacQueen attributes Scottish neglect of her own linguistic and literary traditions to being 'inhibited by . . . English dominance' in such areas (MacQueen 1971); so too in the United States.

Whatever Webster or Fenimore Cooper might assert, and despite the 'bombastic elevation' (as the *Edinburgh Review* called it) with which Joel Barlow endowed his enormous *Columbiad* of 1807, the linguistic and literary standards of most influential Americans long retained a firmly British orientation. As James Russell Lowell put it in 1848, berating his fellow Americans in *A Fable for Critics*:

> You steal Englishmen's books and think Englishmen's thought;
> With their salt on her tail your wild eagle is caught;
> Your literature suits its each whisper and motion
> To what will be thought of it over the ocean.

Nor – a point to bear in mind over 'Irish' as a possible designation for the English of Ireland – did the early use of the label 'the American language' ever achieve much currency, despite repeated examples set from Webster to Mencken. Indeed, despite his own espousal of it (as in my earlier quotation from 1800), Webster himself came to see the fundamental unity of English as more worthy of description and development than nationalistically inspired Americanism. Significantly, his great dictionary of 1828 was entitled *An American Dictionary of the English Language*.

True, this has not inhibited politicians in fits of nationalist fervour from continuing to raise the question of nomenclature from time to time – especially in state legislatures as distinct from Congress.

Indeed there is one state in which the issue has been enshrined in the law of the land (Mencken 1963). This results from a bill introduced by a Chicago legislator named Frank Ryan (interestingly – if obviously – of Irish ancestry) and the law as duly 'enacted by the People of the State of Illinois' in 1923 states, after an appropriate pre-ambular fanfare, that 'The official language of the State of Illinois shall be known hereafter as the "American" language and not as the "English" language.'

This is of course not merely exceptional: it is of little more than anecdotal interest and something of which most Americans (probably not least in Illinois) are totally unaware. American nationhood is mature enough and secure enough not to need the moral prop of a nationally defined, nationally labelled, nationally prescribed national language, 'entire of itself', in Donne's famous words: a linguistic frontier. But that is not to say that the English of the United States is not established as a distinctive vehicle, expressive of American nationhood, policy and culture: a great American novelist like Faulkner could adhere to American literary and linguistic standards as unerringly as a great French novelist like Proust could adhere to French ones.

So too we see nationhood clearly establishing itself in Australia, New Zealand and elsewhere, each country developing naturally its own variety of English, adequate for expressing national aspirations but without the strident pomp and divisiveness that might attend the designation of a national language.

And such developments have equally taken place without recourse to national academies. The English-speaking peoples have traditionally been averse to anything that smacks of linguistic engi-neering, or indeed to any very deeply felt relation between language and nationalism. This is confirmed by the rarity of the exceptions and even, for that matter, by their vociferousness. One thinks of Richard Verstegan (*A Restitution of Decayed Intelligence*, 1605) striving to whip up pride in English nationality through pride in the antiquity of the English tongue – sadly corrupted by the Normans and by quislings like Chaucer. One thinks of the way in which such attacks on Norman-French 'impurities' in English came to be used in the middle of the seventeenth century to attack the royalists and the King's prerogative. One thinks of Daniel Defoe in 1702 proposing to set up an Academy 'to polish and refine' our language, since the 'English Tongue is a Subject not at all less worthy the Labour of such a Society than the French.'

But we would have none of it. There tends to be a note of superior scorn in Anglo-Saxon attitudes to national academies, though the achievements of such institutions as the Académie Française and the Academia Española are far greater than we generally recognize. It is not that they have been querulously and pathetically impotent, taking up a ridiculous Canute-like posture before the waves of linguistic change (cf. Caput 1972). The point is rather that their goals are fundamentally alien to the English-speaking peoples' way of looking at language. A moment's comparison of the relation between British and American English on the one hand with that between Peninsular Spanish and the Spanish of Latin America will bring this out. Not only do the Spanish-speaking republics across the Atlantic have academies matching that of Spain, but in the face of the natural tendency towards some separate linguistic development in the different countries (sometimes encouraged and exploited for nationalistic ends), all these academies have joined forces in a federation. This has been in operation since 1951. Their first purpose, 'to work assiduously for the . . . unity . . . of our common language', would be unexceptionable in a Commonwealth and Anglo-American context (though of course we would dislike the implications of doing anything about it). But to many of us, the second purpose would be totally unacceptable if not incomprehensible: 'to see that its natural growth follows the traditional paths of the Spanish language.'[11] In other words, as with world-wide French, the model and standard are seen as remaining firmly in the historical mother country. And I ought to stress that these words do not proceed from unrepresentative amateurs, ideological enthusiasts, the Spanish-American equivalents of Frank Ryan: they are unquestioningly endorsed by the most sober professional linguists of the countries involved. The intellectual gulf between them and us that I have mentioned can be seen still more clearly in such statements as the following by the two linguists whose report I have used:

> The decisive role that literature fills in the formation of a national language and in the establishment of its literary norm is well known. Hence the preservation and elucidation of the general linguistic norm, as expressed in the literary language, is one of the fundamental tasks of the

[11]The translated 'statute' (1952) is quoted from Guitarte and Quintero 1974.

academies. This work is carried out in the first place by the academy members themselves by participating in their country's life, practising that general linguistic norm in their writings and lending it the prestige of their names. The group of academy members that aspires to represent that which is most select in each nation with regard to letters should constitute a centre of influence for the literary language. This effect, which is difficult to gauge, but whose existence it would be false to deny, is of unfailing importance insofar as it grants value and prestige to the general linguistic norm, in all of a country's cultural activities. (Guitarte and Quintero 1974)

The examples I have been choosing to illustrate the relation between language and nationhood present both close analogies and sharp contrasts with the situation in Scotland.[12] Scotland is a multi-lingual nation, and I have read with great interest something of the important linguistic debate that has gone on in recent years: on nurturing and standardizing the Celtic language of the Gaelic-speaking minority; on bilingual education and broadcasting; on the varieties of language among the Germanic-speaking majority, and in particular on the relation between Scots and Scottish English (McIntosh 1961; 'diglossia' or 'continuum'? – cf. Wood 1977). Scotland has several choices in the adoption of a language policy, and I have tried implicitly to illustrate them through the examples I have been discussing from all over the world.

But there are two points to which I should like to draw attention, both of them factual and non-controversial. We do not have to travel as far as India (where young men in recent years have burned themselves to death on language issues) to see the catastrophic effects of language-based antipathies within a single country: Canada is far enough and Belgium is still closer. Secondly, united flourishing nationhood can subsist without there being a decreed and legally instituted national language. The United States is also a multilingual society, and although there are plenty of problems over linguistic minorities (especially Spanish speakers but more recently also over the moves to recognize Black English), at least neither in law nor in tradition is loyalty to the American flag identified with anything so frighteningly mystical as a national language. And again we have a striking example closer to these islands: Switzerland

---

[12]Nor can I forget that I myself belong to a still smaller nation, basically Celtic but with similar ethnic admixtures to those of Scotland. A patrial Manxman, I learned to sing the Manx National Anthem – in English, and to regard 'God Save the King' as rather sombrely remote from my Manx identity.

functions as an enviably model nation in many respects, social as well as economic – and it is a multilingual nation without a national language.

I could be tempted to argue a more basic and still more solemn case. Nationhood is a precious thing, but language is still more precious. Both are means by which mankind binds itself in communities, but it is by language that mankind actually communicates, and language takes precedence not merely historically but in the personal development and daily life of the individual. Nationhood can help a man fulfil himself: but language is veritably a precondition of fulfilment. Through the faculty of language, moreover, man has relations not merely within the micro-unit of the family but in ever-increasing circles within the street, the village, the district, the county, the nation, the group of neighbouring nations: in principle, quite indefinitely, as widely as mankind itself is spread.

While it is an obvious truth that nations could not exist without languages, it is a more relevant truth that languages could – and did – exist without nations. They did, and perhaps they will again, as we grope towards a more rational, less divisive, and – one hopes – more peaceful destiny for mankind. I will say nothing about the widely-held view that the rhetoric of national unity is the rhetoric of international estrangement.[13] I will however venture to deplore the raising of linguistic frontiers to match the national ones. Beyond question, we must respect every man's mother tongue, nurture it, and help him to find fulfilment through it. But to me it is equally beyond question that the modern world needs to provide this same 'everyman' with a language of wider communication beyond whatever limits are set by his mother tongue – and especially beyond the limits set by his nation.[14] Those nations are

[13]Many nineteenth-century thinkers (such founders of Marxism as Engels among them) already clearly foresaw the darker side of nationalism while fully supporting the cause of oppressed peoples. John Stuart Mill(1849) saw the movement as inherently antisocial, indifferent to everything 'save that which is called by the same name and speaks the same language as themselves. These feelings are characteristic of barbarians.' Instead of a 'levelling tendency which annihilates distinctions and which would have one law, one language, one cosmopolitan character', Southall (1893) noted that nationalism was 'constantly emphasizing distinctions and building up local differences, tending to make languages.'

[14]Not least where the language of his nation is English. We should note the bitterness expressed in Anthony Burgess's *Beard's Roman Women* (1977): 'I remain at the end a monoglot Englishman, unworthy to enter any comity of nations, tied to one tongue as to one cuisine and one insular complex of myths.'

most – not least – fortunate in which the major language of daily currency is already one which (like English, French, Spanish, Arabic) is widely used beyond the frontiers of individual nations. They would in my view be doing a disservice to their own people in attempting to replace it by a language more private and specific to themselves. The Scots of that great literary tradition to which Sir David Lindsay so signally contributed regarded the language of the Scottish nation as English.

References

Alisjahbana, A. T. 1974: 'Language Policy, Language Engineering and Literacy in Indonesia and Malaysia', in Fishman 1974.

Barnes, D. 1974: 'Language Planning in Mainland China: Standardization', in Fishman 1974.

Bawcutt, P. 1976: *Gavin Douglas: A Critical Study*. Edinburgh: Edinburgh University Press.

Beloded, I. 1977: 'The Functioning of National Languages in the USSR under Socialism', in *Problems of the Contemporary World* 50 (ed. L. Gerasimova). Moscow.

Bromage, M. C. 1956: *De Valera and the March of a Nation*. London: Brown, Watson.

Caput, J.-P. 1972: *La Langue française: histoire d'une institution*. Paris: Larousse.

Fishman, J. A. 1971: 'The Impact of Nationalism on Language Planning', in Rubin and Jernudd 1971.

—1973: *Language and Nationalism*. Rowley, Mass.: Newbury House.

—(ed.) 1974: *Advances in Language Planning*. The Hague: Mouton.

Gellner, E. 1964: *Thought and Change*. London: Weidenfeld & Nicolson.

Guitarte, G. L. and Quintero, R. T. 1974: 'Linguistic Correctness and the Role of the Academies in Latin America', in Fishman 1974.

Harries, L. 1976: 'The Nationalization of Swahili in Kenya', *Language in Society* 5.

Haugen, E. 1966: 'Dialect, Language, Nation'. *American Anthropologist* 68.

Kloss, H. 1952: *Die Entwicklung neuer germanischer Kultursprachen von 1800 bis 1959*. Munich: Pohl.

McIntosh, A. 1961: *An Introduction to a Survey of Scottish Dialects*. Edinburgh: Nelson.

Macnamara, J. 1971: 'Successes and Failures in the Movement for the Restoration of Irish', in Rubin and Jernudd 1971.

MacQueen, J. 1971: 'The Case for Early Scottish Literature', in *Edinburgh Studies in English and Scots* (ed. A. J. Aitken *et al.*). London: Longman.

Mencken, H. L. 1963: *The American Language* (ed. R. I. McDavid, Jr). New York: Knopf.

Mill, J. S. 1849: 'The French Revolution and its Assailants'. *Westminster Review*.

Miller, R. A. 1977: *The Japanese Language in Contemporary Japan*. Washington, DC: American Enterprise Inst.

von Polenz, P. 1967: 'Sprachpurismus und Nationalsozialismus', in *Nationalismus in Germanistik und Dichtung* (ed. B. von Wiese and R.Henss). Berlin.

Quirk, R. 1972: *The English Language and Images of Matter*. Oxford: Oxford University Press.

Rubin, J. and Jernudd, B. 1971: *Can Language Be Planned?* Honolulu: East-West Center.

Simon, I. 1961: 'Saxonism Old and New'. *Revue Belge de Philologie et d'Histoire* 39.

Southall, J. E. 1893: *Wales and her Language*. London: Nutt.

Whitely, W. H. 1971: 'Some Factors Influencing Language Policy in Eastern Africa', in Rubin and Jernudd 1971.

Wood, R. E. 1977: 'Potential Issues for Language Planning in Scotland'. *Language Planning Newsletter* 3. Honolulu: East-West Center.

5 Dictionaries

English lexicography knocks Johnnie Walker into a tricuspidal fedora. Over four hundred years, and going stronger than ever.

Of course, in the sixteenth century the market was for 'bilingual' dictionaries (especially Latin-English). We had to wait upon Robert Cawdrey in 1604 for a 'monolingual' model – aimed at 'Ladies . . . or other unskilfull persons'.

But the principles and goals are essentially the same. We don't look up *door* to find that it means the chunk of material that seals off rooms and fridges. We know that. We look up *meretricious* for its meaning, *fuchsia* for its spelling, *controversy* for its pronunciation (to correct somebody else's). The words from Latin (and so forth) today corresponded to the words *in* Latin at the time of Hooker and Shakespeare: the language most familiar to the most educated, least familiar to the least. This is something of an oversimplification, but not all that much. The tradition is rich and unbroken: in Thomas Elyot's Latin dictionary of 1538 we find *aedificium* 'building', in Bullokar's English dictionary of 1616 the minimally anglicised *edifice* 'a building', in the 1979 *Collins, edifice* 'a building'.

For all their bright newness, dictionaries of the 1970s (such as the *Webster Eighth Collegiate*, the *Longman Modern English Dictionary*, the revised *Chambers*, the 6th *Concise Oxford*, the *Longman Dictionary of Contemporary English*, the *Oxford Paperback*) are still basically concerned with translating a relatively foreign language into a relatively familiar one. And – despite the claims of radical differences – there is a striking resemblance between them – as between members of a family. Nor is this specially surprising: however hermetically distinct the financial structure of the publishing firms concerned, the people who actually make the dictionaries are a fairly small group of people who know each other and who are as mobile as musicians. If Solti is with the

Chicago Symphony one week and with the LPO the next, so also do the professional lexicographers like Clarence Barnhart, Sidney Landau and Lawrence Urdang move form one dictionary house to another. Oxford (with R. W. Burchfield and John Sykes) is comparatively stable.

When work began on the new *Collins*, Paul Procter and Della Summers were young conductors under impresario Urdang, and they later moved on to make dictionaries for Longman. Patrick Hanks was recruited to complete the *Collins* when he had finished a somewhat similar job for Hamlyn. Both Urdang and T. H. Long were earlier on the *Random House Dictionary*. All very cosy. But while it desirably makes for shared knowledge and a solid tradition (a euphemism, some would say, for massive reciprocal plagiarism), it is not exactly a prescription for exciting new departures.

Nonetheless, the marketplace demands that for each new dictionary, claims must be made about its uniqueness. For *Collins*, these rest upon coverage (words from wherever 'English is spoken as a native language') and size in relation to provenance (the biggest English dictionary 'to be originated in Britain' since 1933). This is technically true no doubt, though given the American leadership of Urdang (and Long), the American sources that constituted the lexical materials, and in any case the essentially amphi-Atlantic nature of all such enterprises today, the claim is perhaps more one of investment than lexicography. And 'biggest' is by no means as simple a measure as it sounds.

There is certainly some additional coverage, with a fair number of words that I haven't come across in earlier dictionaries – or anywhere else, if it comes to that – for example, *grovet* (wrestling). But the size (nearly twice as 'big' as the *Concise Oxford*) is not primarily on this account. It is achieved in part by including people, places and the like (about one sixth of the whole book, I estimate), and in part by avoiding space-economisers like swung dashes and abbreviations. The latter principle has the laudable aim of making the entries more quickly comprehensible but the cost is considerable – especially in making etymologies (surely used chiefly by readers who can cope with 'OE' and 'OHG') far lengthier than usual: 'from Old French *grouchier* . . . compare Old High German . . .' The former is also for the convenience of Everyman, for whom the dictionary may be his sole reference book.

Combining the dictionary and the encyclopedia is no new idea

(Cockeram did it in 1623), and the distinction between the two types of information is by no means as clear as conventional wisdom would have it. Indeed, it is least satisfactorily upheld by the lexicographers who uphold it most primly. Thus the Oxford and Webster-Merriam tradition is to include *Kafkaesque* but not *Kafka*, though if 'linguistic' principles were strictly observed, only *-esque* ('in the manner of') should be listed. Nor is the distinction any easier to maintain with words having no initial capital. *Collins* defines *motorcycle* as 'a two-wheeled vehicle, having a stronger frame than a bicycle, that is driven by a petrol engine'. Much of this is obviously 'encyclopedic' (indeed incidental), threatening the definition of other words with hair-raising implications which fortunately are not often realized. (We are not told, for instance, that a bus has a larger engine than a car.) The semanticists have long grappled with such problems. What is the *linguistic* meaning of *carrot* or *radio* as distinct from the encyclopedic meaning? We competently choose, use and refer to these things without necessarily knowing that the one is an 'umbelliferous plant' (*Concise*) or that the other 'demodulates electromagnetic waves' (*Collins*). Nor do these 'meanings' help to explain why we can talk of carroty hair or a radio personality.

So *Collins* is sensible enough in effectively dismissing the distinction and putting *Guillaume de Lorris* between *guileless* and *guillemot*. The trouble is knowing where to stop. It is hard enough to establish which words and which meanings of words to list, but if a careful search (especially of other recent dictionaries) gives assurance that every word in yesterday morning's paper will be securely in and adequately defined, the lexicographer has some kind of rough-and-ready guide. But will the names of every *person* and *place* in yesterday's paper provide a similar check? Obviously not: yet on what principle shall we include Margaret Thatcher and Bessie Smith (both in *Collins*) and exclude some John Smith who had to be rescued after a fall in Snowdonia?

The answer is, of course, common sense – and on the whole there seems to have been a good supply in Aylesbury (largely, one gathers, that of Ms Lucy Liddell). Leaders in politics, writing, theatre, music, painting and sport get in; quite a number of relatively obscure figures from the past too (for example, Guiscard, the eleventh-century Norman who became a sort of Sicilian Godfather); and a wide selection of places, from Cottbus on the Spree to Whitehall, both as a street and – I am happy to see – in its metonymic use as (British) Government'.

Goodness knows what is meant by the intriguing claim that 'these items play an increasingly important part in communication today.' The growth of name-dropping? But inevitably in so subjective an area the coverage is uneven, and the chap or the spot you're looking for may not be there. Comics come off worse than straight actors (Harry Lauder makes it but not George Robey, Tommy Handley, or Morecambe and Wise). So in other fields. Bobby Charlton is in; Geoff Boycott isn't. Piggott but not Carson. John Williams (the guitarist) but not Shirley. Healey but not Howe. John le Carré but not Naipaul or Storey. Bud Powell but not Sandy. We even have Bovril but not Oxo. Pink Floyd but not the Hallé Orchestra. The Rolling Stones but not the Amadeus Quartet.

These last examples are more than incidental in their suggestion of trendiness. Bob Dylan gets eight lines; Dylan Thomas four. George Solti, Colin Davis, Janet Baker and Joan Sutherland are all treated with tightlipped and austere brevity as compared with Ringo Starr, Paul McCartney and Mick Jagger.

Even where relatively lavish space is given to unquestionably significant people, it is not so unquestionable whether the space has been well used. Writers and composers tend to have their works listed, directory fashion, rather than their work assessed. For example, Shakespeare gets 20 lines, but 14 of these consist of titles.

Yet the content of entries – whether encyclopedic or lexical – is clearly something to which the editorial team have given great attention. Two claims are made for the special quality of definitions: that they are in 'lucid prose' (p. xv), reflecting progress made in the study of semantics (p. vii); and that they are ordered with priority for the sense that is 'most common in current usage'.

The first of these certainly represents a desirable goal. How well it is achieved is another mater. My impression is that the editors have been more successful with concretes than with abstracts and attributes: the definition of *engine* is shorter, easier and more effective than the one in the *Concise Oxford*. On the other hand, the converse seems true for the adjective *enervate*: 'lacking vigour' (*Concise*); 'deprived of strength' (*Collins*), with an unfortunate and unwanted suggestion of some external agency. But for the most part, I doubt whether the defining skills are better or worse than in the general run of recent dictionaries, and despite the claims about freshening things up, one is struck by the survival of the most traditional type of defining language. Often *ignotum per ignotius*. Take *anus*. The first dictionary I ever used (and still go back to occasionally: Ogilvie-Annandale in a 'new' edition of 1895) at least justifies its 'inferior opening of the alimentary canal' by first putting something a bit more straighforward. The *Concise Oxford* has only 'terminal excretory opening of alimentary canal' – which isn't going to help the scared patient trying to make sense of something he heard the doctor say about his piles. *Collins* offers no breakthrough: 'the excretory opening at the end of the alimentary canal'. The reader who understands the words in definitions like these is unlikely to be ignorant of the words they define. This is a trap laid not merely by the centuries-old fustian tradition but also by the lexicographer's neglect of recent work in semantics and lexicology. By contrast, in the *Longman Dictionary of Contemporary English*, Paul Procter insisted on all words being defined within a restricted vocabulary, and this had the predictable effect of extracting elemental meaning in the simplest language. In consequence, *anus* is defined as 'the hole through which solid food waste leaves the bowels'.

The second of the defining characteristics is more controversial. There are three fairly obvious choices in handling polysemous words. First, lay out the meanings in the order which is most explanatory semantically. This is the least popular option, doubtless because it is most demanding. But the second is in effect closely similar: lay out the meanings in historical order (thus frequently explaining how one meaning has developed from an earlier more 'basic' one). This is the principle largely adopted by Merriam-Webster, and the most serious objection to it is that it can obviously entail giving priority to a meaning that is now relatively unimportant. My favourite example is *sad* in *Chambers* ('entirely new edition' 1972), on which see p. 95 below.

The third way is the one claimed for both the *Concise Oxford* and the new *Collins*: 'commonest meaning first'. Superficially attractive for obvious reasons, this is probably the least satisfactory of the three. There is no technique currently available to establish frequency of meanings – even if we could agree on the principles and the type of discourse to be used for the inquiry. (For example, there must be plently of people for whom *ticket* has 'parking summons' as the commonest meaning in 'I got a ticket', but 'theatrical admission' in 'I've got some tickets'.) This is perhaps fortunate, since the principle would produce chaotically mystifying dictionary entries if it were seriously applied. But of course it isn't. The *Collins* definition of *paper* begins with the 'substance made from cellulose fibres' (and not, say, with the sense of 'today's paper'). The definition of *crane* begins with 'long-legged wading bird', and I would bet that there aren't many people for whom the 'lifting machine' isn't commoner. The treatment of *crash* begins with the acoustic sense, though the compounds that follow (like *crash barrier, crash helmet*) might sufficiently suggest that the 'destructive impact' sense is linguistically dominant.

But I don't want these remarks to sound too negative. For all that we may react against the brash stridency with which publishers plug 'big is beautiful' and 'new is great', the brisk market for dictionaries is healthy for lexicography. Signs of originality and progress are far more modest than blurbs and forewords would suggest, but they are real. And this is more true of the new *Collins* than of some other recent dictionaries. For a long time, 'dictionary' has meant 'Oxford' in this country almost as automatically as it has meant (the far more polysemous) 'Webster' in the United States. Oxford deserves its fine reputation – and, if for no other reason, it equally deserves more insistent competition that it has been used to. The various alternative approaches now being pressed by such houses as Longman and Collins will have a beneficial effect upon lexicography as a whole.

6 'Dr Murray, Oxford'

The fascination of the pilgrimage lies in the feeling of physical contact with what we revere. A year or so ago, I visited Mill Hill School, seeking relics of the patriarchal James Murray: few in all conscience (a portrait, the reconstructed 'scriptorium', the house he lived in) but enough to kindle the imagination and to establish (if only by staring across the still miraculously rural landscape that uplifted him) a sense of continuity with the 1870s when he taught and wrote there.

The urge to seek palpable signs of continuity was strong in Murray, too. He sat a couple of his children on the knee of a man who had witnessed Napoleon's surrender in 1815; as a child himself, he marvelled at meeting old Mrs Penn who had known Sir Walter Scott (and at talking to a man who had talked to a man who had heard the proclamation of William and Mary in 1689). His granddaughter has apparently inherited just such an urge, and no small part of her achievement is the able way in which a powerful sense of continuity is communicated.

Elisabeth Murray was five when the great man died, and has clear memories of him that go back a couple of years before this, thoroughly conscious of his greatness before ever she watched in 1913 the splendid procession when he (and Thomas Hardy) received the Cambridge Litt.D. As with most of his honours, this was, of course, to acknowledge his long and distinguished service to lexicography, which, by then, had brought the *Oxford English Dictionary* within sight of completion. But although he might not otherwise have received such honours (or been the subject of a major biography), one of the things that emerges clearly from Miss Murray's book is

Note: This chapter first appeared as a review of *Caught in the Web of Words: James A. H. Murray and the 'Oxford English Dictionary'* by K. M. Elisabeth Murray, published in *The Listener*, 20 October 1977.

that his greatness existed quite independently of his Herculean labours on the dictionary. For me, at any rate, the story of the first half of his life (before his involvement with the dictionary) is even more impressive than the story of part two, when the dictionary looms over everything, almost *is* everything.

At the age of 12, when the one-teacher, one-room village school closed because of a severe cholera outbreak, he took a job for six months as a cowherd at two shillings a month (with his keep), and used what leisure he had to work away at his Latin – despite teasing from the other farmhands. Among his other accomplishments by this time were a fair knowledge of Chinese characters (begun at seven), the Hebrew alphabet (still earlier), some astronomy, and considerable botany. He had, for instance, mastered the Linnaean taxonomy and had compiled a nine-volume herbarium. After the epidemic, and until he was 14, he attended the school at Minto, walking a mile and a half each way, barefoot in summer. This completed his formal education by providing him with algebra, chemistry, physics (electricity and the mechanics of steam power), and four more languages – French, Italian, German and Greek.

Any further education had to be by his own efforts: there were few books in the house, and little money from his father's tailoring trade to buy any; and not being the son of a 'feuar', he was denied access even to the modest resources of the local library. Yet with what neighbourly help he could get, he acquired a staggering number and degree of skills (book-binding, land-surveying, tailoring – he made his own trousers till he was 27), as well as perfecting his German and Greek. All this while he earned a bit at farmwork.

So impressive was this self-education that, at 17, he was appointed one of the three teachers at Hawick United School. On top of a crowded teaching programme, he managed to find time for a multiplicity of other educational and cultural work. For example, he helped to found the Hawick Archaeological Society (whose proceedings are still published annually), catalogued the rapidly increasing finds, and kept the minute book – which shows him contributing an original paper at almost every meeting: from local earthworks to onomastics, from the Norse discovery of America to the contribution of philology in the history of Western Europe.

At the age of 20, he was sufficiently recognized locally as a prodigy to be offered the post of headmaster in the Hawick Academy. And on and on goes the success story: his revolutionarily liberal methods as teacher, dispensing with the 'tawze' to instil far more, far faster, by his infectious enthusiasm and the obvious profundity of his knowledge. He was Liberal, too, in politics, with deep concern for the appalling slums proliferating in the rapid industrial growth of Hawick; and when he joined in welcoming Louis Kossuth to Hawick, he had learned enough Hungarian to astonish this freedom-fighter with a slogan in his own language. Indeed, by then, he could have managed the like for an Arab, a Hindu, a Hottentot and even a Tongan. And he had introduced Graham Bell to the mysteries of electricity, thus becoming (as Bell later put it) the 'grandfather of the telephone'.

One anecdote shows how extraordinary was this tall, athletic young man with flowing beard (he never shaved), and how readily a total stranger could be impressed by him, with his brilliance and potential. One June when he was 24, he crossed the Cheviots to attend a learned meeting in Alnwick, and attracted Canon Greenwell of Durham by the sharpness of his observations on Anglo-Saxon. When he learned from Murray that all this had been acquired without ever having access to the source materials, the canon sent off a box of rare and valuable books from his own and the Durham Cathedral Library. Murray was so delighted that before he returned the books (Hooker, Thwaites, the Heptateuch, the Durham Gospels), he made complete transcripts in several cases, so that he could have his own copies. Forty years later, he was still using them as he worked on the *OED* in the Banbury Road, because they saved him the trouble of visiting the Bodleian when he needed to check a reference.

But the journey from Roxburghshire to Oxford was in no way as logical and inevitable as this youthful growth might suggest. It lay via London, where Murray moved in a vain attempt to keep his wife alive in a warmer climate, via a city bank where he earned a living through his ability to handle foreign correspondence, via the BM every Saturday afternoon where he recuperated from the bank's intellectual aridity, and via University College London, and the fort-nightly meetings there of the Philological Society. These took place in an atmosphere of enormous academic excitement: Furnivall, Ellis, Skeat, Prince Louis Bonaparte, R. G. Latham and a dozen others were bundling English scholars on to the philological band-wagon that had been rolling impressively in Germany for over a genera-tion. Indeed, Edward Arber makes it clear in a letter of 1873

that the flourishing university study of English that was to be taken
for granted in the 20th century owed its development to a handful of
scholars, Murray among them.

Among other things, F. J. Furnivall had roped him into the editing
of early literary material for the Early English Text Society, itself a
response to the need for making mediaeval works available for lexicographers engaged in the *New* (later *Oxford*) *English Dictionary* –
the ambitious project conceived by the Philological Society in the
late 1850s. But Murray's was no mere bookish interest in linguistics.
By the time he (unsuccessfully) applied for a job in the BM, he could
claim a knowledge of nearly 30 tongues, and was praised by Henry
Sweet for his 'keen appreciation of living language'. While still teaching himself to be a teacher, in fact, he recognized that his pupils' 'bad'
grammar was the 'good' grammar of Scots – and around 1860 he
wrote a book to prove it, although it was never published.

It was through the Philological Society, too, that he met the headmaster of Mill Hill and was persuaded, despite a drop in salary, to
take a teaching post there – very happily in the event. His years at
Mill Hill (1870-85) he came to call his 'Arcadian time', the happiest
period of his life. The school itself had been through a bad period,
and numbers went up from 34, when he joined the staff, to 183 by
1878, in no small measure through his energy and dedication. By this
year, too, he had already (through Furnivall, Sweet, and his editing
for the EETS) become deeply involved in the dictionary project and
was about to take on – with great misgivings – the role of editor.

But he had other preoccupations in the early Mill Hill years – raising a family (eventually 11) with his new wife, and worrying over
academic qualifications to help him keep his end up with the other
teachers at Mill Hill – none of whom, of course, was in the same
class as Murray, even as teachers, let alone as scholars. Nonetheless,
worry he did, and this involved simultaneously studying for an external London BA and lobbying for an honorary doctorate from
Edinburgh, both with success. So it was that the London University
registrar was asked in 1874 by a new BA if he might attend the
capping ceremony wearing the robes of an Edinburgh LLD. 'He was
not,' his granddaughter demurely observes, 'above a little understandable vanity.' He was not indeed. Much later in the book, she
quotes a report on his Glasgow degree (1896) when he presented
himself astonishingly arrayed in four hoods of earlier degrees 'by
way of compliment,' as he explained it, 'to the university that was

giving him yet another'.

It was, of course, above all, his work on the dictionary that brought these honours (and in addition a Civil List pension in 1884, a knighthood in 1908, and even an Oxford doctorate in 1914: 'At last!' exclaimed his wife); and it is naturally to the tangled and often embittered struggles over the dictionary that Miss Murray devotes most of her attention and space. As well she might. Even while the dictionary was a part-time enterprise at Mill Hill, its reputation brought droves of visitors from the continent and the United States (as well as from nearer home: Gladstone 'made a habit of dropping in') F. J. Child of Harvard told friends that there were three things that must be seen by any American visitor to London: and the other two were the Tower and Westminster Abbey.

Although the chronology requires the reader's patience in unravelling (and there are quite a few editorial blemishes such as the occasional lost or misplaced note), the author handles the complex material very ably, and tells a highly readable and entertaining story from first to last. Her source materials were voluminous, and their examination and assessment must have constituted an extremely arduous task.

The ebullient and unconventional Furnivall comes out of it badly (vain, unprincipled, outspokenly anti-religion and pro-sex, opportunistic, unscholarly – though no one contributed more quotations for the dictionary), and the Clarendon Press less well than its officers and delegates perhaps deserve. But this is not because Miss Murray makes out that her grandfather was faultless. His style of writing often showed poor taste – and he had almost no taste at all for literature in his reading. He could be vain, disingenuous, domineering, sententious, a bit paranoid; he could get 'almost hysterical' with his poor colleagues, Bradley and Craigie; and (as we see repeatedly) 'enjoyed a certain sense of martydom.' But she shows, too, that he enjoyed a sense of humour. He was fond of repeating an alleged dream in which Boswell asked Johnson: 'What would you say, Sir, if you were told that in a hundred years' time a bigger and better dictionary than yours would be compiled by a Whig?' Johnson grunted. 'A Dissenter.' Johnson stirred in his chair. 'A Scotsman.' Johnson began, 'Sir. . .' but Boswell persisted – ' and that the University of Oxford would publish it.' 'Sir,' thundered Johnson, 'in order to be facetious it is not necessary to be indecent.'

Miss Murray can be forgiven for being somewhat partisan in

insisting on Furnivall's mischief-making, the philistinism of the Press, the apathy of the Philological Society, since we are so easily persuaded of how uniquely indebted we are to him. Indispensability is a rare quality, but it is one we can confidently attribute to James Murray: without him we can be quite sure that we would not have had the *OED* as we know it. He had a tough struggle to evolve and establish basic principles of lexicography that we now take for granted: above all, the lexicographer's theoretical objectivity – deriving his definitions from the analysis of his data and not merely using citations to illustrate meanings assumed aprioristically. And on top of that, in the evolutionary climate of the time, to trace the history of every word and meaning that had ever been in use during the long centuries since 1150.

The task alone, even in the best of circumstances, would have daunted into inactivity a lesser man. And Murray's circumstances were in many ways appalling. Texts were still being edited, let alone being read for citations, when he was already working on the early letters of the alphabet, so that he faced for many years the frightening situation of a sorcerer's apprentice: as slips were removed for completed letters, there were still more slips awaiting attention than he had had at the outset. The work was no mere compilation: nearly every article entailed totally original research, and a single word could take many weeks, while for years no delegation of the research was possible.

He undertook a massive daily workload: even in his late seventies, the ordeal of an 80 or 90-hour week was normal, the day's work beginning at 6am or earlier, in a cold, damp, corrugated iron hut which (till the stove got the air tolerable) forced him to work with his feet in a box. He was haunted by a very real poverty, often working at a net annual loss, dipping into his savings to pay assistants, depending on loans to keep the work going – and on gifts from friends in order to take his family on holidays. The only pocket-money his children ever had was for sorting dictionary slips.

He had to fight prejudices and preconceptions that we can scarcely imagine: that words – let alone citations – should be only from 'good' authors; that there must be no slang, no dialect, no coarseness, no recent coinage which an august delegate or pedantic correspondent considered jargon (he was driven to omit *appendicitis*, for example). He had to jolly along the worldwide network of volunteers who sent in the basic material (one of the most dedicated turned out to be a Broadmoor inmate) to 'Dr Murray, Oxford'. Above all, he felt constantly hounded to keep down the scale of the dictionary (which the delegates feared – with some justification – was in danger of becoming a millstone large enough to sink the entire Clarendon enterprise); and his firm belief that his work was undervalued and uncomprehended prevented him from getting on to a colleaguely footing with his publishers.

His shade is probably deriving grim satisfaction from the fact that his granddaughter's biography of him is published by Yale. And although he strongly disapproved of biography, he would surely have enjoyed this one: the keenly-drawn vignettes of his contemporaries; being reminded of the coarsely unhelpful 'birth control' advice the oft-pregnant Ada was given by her doctor ('slide down the stairs headfirst on your stomach'); being reminded, too, that the sole evidence for the use of *anamorphose* in the *OED* is J. A. H. Murray, writing in the Mill Hill school magazine; the feeling of disgrace to a devoutly Nonconformist family when his son Aelfric decided to become a C of E parson. Would even so capacious a memory as his have retained the detail that, when he started writing with the middle initials that he had adopted, he hadn't decided what to make them stand for?

7 Setting New Word Records

If you are looking for comfortable reassurance in a world of headlong heedless change, there is always the English dictionary. There are few more firmly established and dependably stable institutions. Some of the reasons for this are less reassuring.

New dictionaries are extremely expensive to produce. Even starting with generations of expertise and rich collections of data, Merriam-Webster had to invest $3,500,000 in their most recent full-scale dictionary, the *Third International* of 1961. And equally unlike the magnificent government-funded *Trésor de la langue française* at Nancy, the other major dictionary enterprises in the English-speaking world (Random House and Heritage in the United States, for example; Oxford and Longman in Britain) depend on success in the market-place to recoup investment. And with so much to recoup, it is understandable if tried and trusty models are retained and the heady spirit of adventure firmly discouraged, as the industry sells hard to achieve (with considerable success) its goal of getting a dictionary into every home. Dictionary A cannot afford to omit information of the kind in Dictionary B: cannot even risk getting out on a thin commercial limb by treating it too differently.

This, of course, has the reflexive effect of establishing even more firmly in the public mind what is to be expected of and in a dictionary – even to arcane symbols indicating parts of speech and etymologies which it is hard to believe the average home attempts to decode. The time-hallowed format helps to place it mentally with the Bible (alongside which it is likely to find itself physically), and the advertiser's warning that 'no home should be without it' finds a ready response in the natural awe that we rightly have for our

Note: This chapter first appeared in *The Times Literary Supplement* No. 3893, 22 October 1976.

language faculty and further contributes to the implicit belief that the dictionary is one's linguistic bible. Implicit? Explicit often enough, as in the review of *Third International* by the Right Reverend R. S. Emrich, who claims that Webster has forsaken 'its post as the guardian of our language.' This is quoted by J. H. Sledd and W. R. Ebbitt in *Dictionaries and That Dictionary* (1962), which analyses the (largely hostile) reception of the *Third International* and contributes one of the few examinations that we have in English of the dictionary as an institution and of the criteria by which dictionaries can be assessed.

Having thus, over a couple of centuries, striven to make the public dictionary-conscious, lexicographers are now in the position of sorcerer's apprentice, with a public demanding buckets to be refilled with the same sort of material in the same way.

If this is not bad enough, the third reason for the stability of the dictionary model is that, bluntly, there has been insufficient development in lexicological theory since the time of Samuel Johnson and Noah Webster (or indeed their predecessors) for radical change in lexicography to be worth contemplating.

J. R. Hulbert, Craigie's collaborator on the *Dictionary of American English*, wrote in 1955 of lexicography as being 'more enjoyable' than most research because 'one does not devote days, months, or even years to testing an hypothesis only to decide that it is not tenable.' Does not, and, tacitly, has no need to. This has great advantages for continuity, of course: Hulbert is right that the great *Oxford English Dictionary* is 'all of a piece' precisely because the technique was to apply an approach 'which in all essentials was to prove quite satisfactory for the work of fifty years.'

In brief, the theory is this. A language has at a given time a finite inventory of words, the meanings of which are revealed in the course of general usage. Since the lexicographer is as liable to be as deviant as the next man, he must have recourse to the usage of as many people as he can – in print. This last phrase embodies the proud ideal of descriptive objectivity; his citations (and interpretations of them) are publicly verifiable. True, in some cases it is possible to infer the meaning from the etymology (*bibliophile* for example, if you know the Greek *biblion* 'book' and *philos* 'loving'), and this is one of the reasons that dictionaries always supply etymologies. It also helps to account for one of the most pernicious of popular *idées fixes*: that this gives you the 'real' meaning and that if it differs from modern everyday usage, it only goes to show how corrupt the language has become. But for the professional lexicographer, definitions are based not on etymology or 'on an editor's idea of what words ought to mean but rather on the meanings actually given to words by [those] who use them' (*6,000 Words: A Supplement to Webster's Third New International Dictionary* (1976)).

The constraints and limitations of this practice are no less obvious than its advantages. Print represents an infinitesimal fraction of language use: new words, new senses, special nuances usually occur first (perhaps only) in speech. But the sentence heard in a bar is not verifiable: the printed example has scholarly respectability in having a quotable accessible source. So a century after sound recordings (30 years after cheap recording on tape and the like) became possible, the lexicographer continues to restrict his sources to the tiny printed sample. Common sense of course often ensures that a lexicographer who 'knows' a word or meaning will embark on special searches of the printed record to make sure it gets in – but, needless to say, this is turning the theory on its head.

Yet this is now taken so much for granted, self-evidently the only respectable lexicographical procedure, that while proclaiming the truism that a dictionary must 'keep up with the living language' (*6,000 Words*), it seems no contradiction a page or so later to find a word's getting 'into the language' equated with meeting it 'in print'.

A further advantage of print however is sometimes argued. While wanting to be up to date, a lexicographer is aware that many usages in ordinary conversation (a daring metaphor, a slipshod substitute for the *mot juste* that refuses to come to mind at the required moment, a slip of the tongue, a word used in a sense special to a family or other private group) never become widely established in the language. Wait for them to get into print, the argument goes, and you can tell the men from the boys. Quite apart from there being no clear idea of how *widely* established a word has to be, or of what 'established' means, the argument of course is very shaky. Given the prestige conferred by originality, print is a positive and highly convenient breeding-ground for words or meanings that were never heard before they were written. Given further the tendency to take citations from the more prestigious authors, it is not difficult to see the danger of a highly skewed lexicon emerging from principles designed precisely in the interests of objective generality. Thus the *OED Supplement* (1972) has a policy of 'liberally representing the vocabulary of such writers as Kipling, Yeats, James Joyce, and Dylan Thomas', even though this means entries for *hapax legomena* like Beckett's *athambia*.

But then arises a further argument in favour of print. Back to 'widely established' again. Although no dictionary can afford to parade this very prominently, the aim is not really to record *all* the words and meanings current in English: no attempt is made to include local dialect, much of the slang, occupational specialities (though those of the miner and bricklayer are more likely to fall under this restriction than those of the doctor or artist), and so on. For the most part, print aims at being communicable across dialectal and professional boundaries and is thus a safer source of data. The further this line is pressed, of course, the shakier becomes the claim that modern lexicography provides unbiased description, far from the normative, subjective hand of Grundyism: it is self-confessedly selective, biased, tending to describe (and hence, for the user, prescribe) the norms not of the language at large but of writers and editors who are deliberately aiming at their *idea* of norms.

Nor can restriction to printed sources avoid the dialectal, slang, and occupational terms which it is not the purpose of the dictionary to register: every dictionary needs to have labels like 'colloq.', 'sl.', 'legal' etc., to specify the limited currency of such items that have leaked in through print – since of course print includes novels and plays, which in the interests of realism contain their authors' filtered views of norms in these areas. The dangers of moving still further from an objective linguistic record are again obvious, and R. W. Burchfield mentions his entries of dialect words from Lawrence (e.g. *barkle*) and Joyce (e.g. *baw-ways*) in the *OED Supplement*.

Now when a novelist, trying to mime uneducated speech (not, let us hope, entirely from his imagination), writes ' "I ain't got no dough to buy a ticket," said the urchin', the lexicographer who is working to rule ties up *urchin* (perhaps also *ain't*) with the double negative, and feels justified in appending some such label as 'slang' to this use of *dough* (with *buy*, as distinct from *bake*). It is a poor source for contemporary slang, but let that pass. But when Dwight Macdonald, knowing (as a native speaker knows) just how slangy the word is, none the less interpolates it into an otherwise fully orthodox sentence, he intends the stylistic misfit to be noticed. The lexicographer (still working to rule) feels obliged to ignore his own private sensibility and records this as an apparent instance of *dough* 'money' being no longer slang. In this (a true story: see Sledd and Ebbitt, 261), we see how insecure are the foundations of modern lexico-graphical procedures.

Let me make it clear that I am not knocking dictionaries. I love them; I own dozens; I am proud of the achievement of the English-speaking countries in this great industry; I inspect with delight each major new model as it rolls off the production lines. I admire the well-organized enterprises and their intelligent dedicated staffs. I am not even particularly jealous that reviewers give so much more space to *dictionaries* than to *grammars* of English. I can truthfully say that many of my best friends are lexicographers. I am old enough to have a pathetic belief in progress and in the advancement of science (in linguistics as in the improvement of hair sprays). But looking for progress in lexicography over the past century or so does little to sustain such faith.

I still possess the first dictionary I ever saw – an Ogilvie in a prominently trumpeted 'New Edition' of 1895 by Annandale (in fact basically of much older vintage) and certainly regarded as still new enough to be the domestic dictionary in a thrifty household through the 1920s. Dr Ogilvie had in fact given British lexicography a decisive new direction about 1850 by importing features from the American tradition. I was captivated by nice grey illustrations of such mysteries as *gabions*, *oak galls*, and *galvanic batteries*. There were nine fascinating lines encapsulating *Darwinism*; contrast the laconic line and a half in the latest *Concise Oxford*, 500 pages longer – but of course Darwin means much less in the 1970s than it meant for Ogilvie-Annandale.

It contained *piss* ('To discharge urine') but not *shit* or any of the other ordinary names for relevant parts, functions, or operations that one was finding of increasing interest. It later transpired that *vulva* was there (and *anus*: 'inferior opening of the alimentary canal'), but how was a semi-literate boy of ten to know? The defining strategy was sometimes heavy going. '*Coquettish a*. Pertaining to a coquette or coquetry' necessarily involved looking up *pertaining*, which wasn't in, and then *pertain*, '*vi*; after five lines of inflection and etymology (referring me to Latin *teneo* 'whence also *tenant*, *contain*') this began the list of meanings with 'to belong', which was less than helpful. There were enthralling appendixes giving such data as the currencies of every country on earth and telling me how to address 'ceremonious communications' to a state governor in the

United States, the Lord Lieutenant of Ireland (quite intricate), or an MP (easy, since 'not specially recognized').

It is worth noting that even the 1971 printing of the latest unabridged Webster still contains such information, including the arresting injunction which I quote in its mysterious entirety:

duke's eldest son's eldest son use grandfather's third title

And apropos of illustrations, although all but half a dozen of the full-page ones were dropped between 1961 and 1971, two of these are devoted to ships: incredibly, both to the intricacies of *sailing* ships – schooners and fully rigged three-masters.

Such deliberate (or merely unconsidered?) conservatism contrasts oddly with strident claims to 'newness', as insistent with the latest models of Webster, *Chambers* (1973) and *Concise Oxford* (1976) as it was with Ogilvie-Annandale (1895). In what, when we get down to it, does the newness inhere? Well, for one important thing, there is great progress in readability: typography and layout are more attractive and more efficient. And a great deal of valuable thought has been given to refining the policy with definitions. Where Ogilvie-Annandale has *appalling* as 'adapted to appal', Dr Sykes in the new *COD* (its predecessor had no separate definition) has the limpid 'shocking, unpleasant': though for *anus* he is stodgily Latinate with 'terminal excretory opening of alimentary canal'.

Again, new editions are quick to incorporate the latest information on etymology (especially now in the light of C. T. Onions *et al.*, *Oxford Dictionary of Etymology*, 1966). They are in general more careful and more sensitive with 'usage labels' (Dr Sykes calls the use of *appalling* that I have quoted 'colloq.'), but this is itself a sensitive issue and in recent years the Webster dictionaries have sought to play down their prescriptive role by using such labels very sparingly: the *Third International* and the derived *Eighth Collegiate* (1976 printing) leave *appalling* without any stylistic restrictions. Even *wop* 'Italian', which *COD* labels 'derog.', is more tentatively restricted in the Websters as only *usually* 'used disparagingly'.

This is part of a more general development: the striving towards objectivity and descriptive humility, weaning the public from their search for magisterial authority in a dictionary. It is doubtless most obvious in the way no lexical censorship is any longer exercised, and lexicographers point proudly to their liberal admission of all the naughty words that Dr Johnson archly accused his lady critics of searching for. But this permissiveness is in fact little to boast of. In the first place, it results from no deepthroated roar at the barricades: lexicographers are merely following, from the secure distance of a decade (still more cautiously in the United States), the licensed admission of these words in fiction and other printed as well as oral material. In any case, no new lexicological principle is involved, indeed no 'new' information is being revealed; and it could even be argued that dictionaries are now merely pandering to current waves of full-frontal fashion. Unevenly at that: A. M. Macdonald's *Chambers* (1973) and the new *COD* list the more notorious items, but not neccessarily all the colloquial periphrases: no *hard-on*, for example, which is in the Webster *Collegiate*. Webster themselves, however, seem to be in considerable sexual disarray. Already in the 1961 printing of the *Third, cunt* was included; but *fuck* was not, and it did not appear in the Addenda of 1971 or in the new separately published supplement *6,000 Words* (1976). The *Seventh Collegiate*, derived from the *Third International*, had neither *cunt* nor *fuck* in 1972, but the *Eighth* had both in 1973. It appears that the *Seventh* is in fact being kept in print for supply to institutions that don't like their dictionaries to mix up bed and board. By contrast, Oxford spelled out with scholarly precision its new policy in relation to such taboos in an article by R. W. Burchfield (*The Times Literary Supplement*, 13 October 1972).

But the chief criterion of newness is the number of new words recorded, and setting new records in this direction is rather like putting the weight, with each competitor free to decide what weight to throw. Here is where the market competition and the absence of advanced lexicological theory interact with the worst effects.

In 1973 Clarence Barnhart and his colleagues produced a *Dictionary of New English 1963-1972*, containing 'words' not previously recorded in standard dictionaries (except those omitted for reasons of delicacy: the morality of this book – if not its catholic source materials and its projected market – is essentially trans-atlantic). As a dictionary, it was unkindly rated by *The Times Literary Supplement* (5 April 1974) 'the silliest yet', and you can see what the reviewer meant. Though providing in the introduction a valuable summary of current lexicographical method, even spelling out to some extent the criteria adopted for recognizing an entity as one of the (new) 'words', it exposed through its very explicitness (and above all by necessarily excluding all the normal words of English) the shaky foundations on which it rested.

Nevertheless, Merriam-Webster have paid Barnhart the compliment of producing a strictly similar volume on a similar scale: *6,000. Words* (1976) – comprising all the 'new words' admitted through their filing and screening system since the 1961 *Third*. Many of the entries seem not so much to bring readers up to date as Merriam themselves: *chutzpah* (Burchfield's *Supplement* has citations from 1892) and *buzz off* (Burchfield has citations from 1914), for example. They even include the time-honoured but not style-honoured *codswallop* – but without a slang label. Of course the 6,000 include many very welcome entries such as *hadal, nebbish, neuristor*, but an embarrassingly high proportion suggest that the numbers game has got out of hand. Totally predictable items involving regular affixation processes help to swell the statistics (*demystify, depollute, denuclearize* and the like). One is grateful not to find a host of 'new' *un*-words also, if left uneasy at the apparent absence of a principle. Again, there are derivatives like *Chomskyan* and *Kafkaesque*, where the only reason for inclusion is the suffixation, though ironically that is the only part that needs no explanation. The semantic interest of such items of course wholly resides in the work of Chomsky and Kafka: but these are people, not words, and their work is material for an encyclopedia not a dictionary.

But the entries that really seem contrived are the scarcely naturalized foreign words such as *Karatzu* (ware), *jun* (a North Korean coin), *objet trouvé*, with nary a theoretical glimpse of the alchemy by which they become part of English; and above all, perhaps, menu items such as *oysters Rockefeller* and the 'compounds' like *gang bang, palazzo pants*, and *sudden infant death syndrome*. New? English? Words?

This should not be read as a criticism of the Merriam team alone but – as is my recurrent theme – of the complacent assumptions in current lexicography. Identical or comparable examples could be given from Barnhart's 1973 dictionary and equally from the first volume of Burchfield's *Supplement*. As well as in *6,000 Words, depollute* is in Barnhart but not in Burchfield, though *denuclearize* (surely a form of depollution) is in all three and in the new *COD* as well. *Watson-Crick*, though a peculiarly British-made 'compound', is in both *6,000 Words* and Barnhart but not in *Chambers*; nor is it in *COD*, whose only *Watson* is Sherlock Holmes's friend, scarely more at principled ease in being listed and glossed as a lexical item. Burchfield has no *Chomskyan*, but he has *Bloomsbury* on the strength of such citations as a D. H. Lawrence letter which speaks of Bloomsbury 'enjoying itself in Paris'. Surely again a linguistic generalization is missed here – not to mention its implications. Where do we stop? 'Watford is peaceful' (place), 'Watford is rioting' (people of Watford), 'Watford is moving up the league' (football team).

Despite this open-house policy, some solemn thinking gets done – and goes wrong. One new 'word' since 1961 that might occur to a reader is *streak* (*-er, -ing*), which is in the new *COD* (though not in *Chambers*). But in their prefatory matter, the Merriam editors explain that it takes more than just a year or so's currency and a well-defined meaning to get into Webster: *streak* is excluded as being among those words that 'enjoy a brief vogue . . . then disappear.' Within days of my reading this, the papers were full of the streaking episode at the Montreal Olympics, and even in Bloomsbury I could feel the glow of Springfield's red faces.

But this example does highlight the problem inherent in Barnhart and *6,000 Words*, and very much in the foreground for general dictionaries like *COD*: what sort of currency must a word or meaning have before speakers of the language recognize it as established? There is something gross about a lexicography which demands *n* occurrences over *t* units of time and which has no means of formally recognizing the misty penumbra that ordinary people are thoroughly conscious of ('if I may so term it,' 'sort of – , as you might say'). The Larousse group (Giraud, Pamart, Riverain) had at least a better metaphor for their volume that is analogous to *6,000 Words* and Barnhart: *Les mots dans le vent* (1971).

And if we are dissatisfied with the admission of new words and meanings, we have every reason to feel likewise over the means by which obsolescence is noted. Again, little explicit theory or even detailed observation is available, but one would expect the death-rate of words and meanings to be rather similar to the birth-rate. In some areas of lexicon, this seems to be an inescapable truism (*landau, victoria, brougham* – out; *convertible, coupé, limousine, fastback* – in).

If a dictionary has as its policy the keeping of a historical record, then of course a word once admitted can never be excluded: since someone may read the (Chaucerian, Miltonian) text in which now obsolete words occur, it is necessary that a dictionary should be to hand that explains them. Thus we have the 13 volumes of the great *Oxford Dictionary*. The policy of the unabridged Webster is equally clear in this respect. It is meanings from 1755 to the present that will be recorded, but in addition are included those 'found in . . . a few major writers' such as Shakespeare: in the light of which principle, of course, the cool-run sense of *streak* should have been included in the 6,000 since its place in the printed literature at some time since 1755 overrules the (inaccurate) claim about its presnt obsolescence.

It is with the shortish desk dictionary of current English that the problem is acute. Should 'current' refer only to the vocabulary in productive use, or should it comprise items in literature (Dickens, Pope, Shakespeare) that members of our current culture are liable to read? The latter position is the one taken up – if a little equivocally – by Dr Sykes in *COD*. But this carries an editorial obligation to label as obsolete any words that are retained for the purposes of reading older literature. Sure enough, *brougham* is both included in *COD* and duly labelled, though *vesta* and *lucifer* (both 'match') are included with no indication that they have long since become obsolete. In some cases, discrimination seems ill-motivated: the beer-measure sense of *pin* has gone from *COD*, but *firkin, hogshead, kilderkin, tierce, puncheon* (which, I am assured by the Brewers' Society, are all rarer than *pin*) are still included. Miss Macdonald's *Chambers* (1973), despite the *Twentieth Century* in its title, provides more striking examples. The entry for the adjective *sad* begins with the meanings 'sated,' 'steadfast,' 'constant,' 'staid,' 'sedate,' 'serious,' 'earnest.' A poor tenth comes 'sorrowful,' with no indication that this meaning has a better twentieth-century track record.

But leaving aside individual editorial slips, my point is that, apart from common sense, there seems no reliable practice of lexical geriatrics, and dictionary makers remain better registrars of births than of deaths. A few hypotheses and experiments in elicitation techniques and informant reactions might well have resulted in disappointment, but (*pace* Professor Hulbert) it is certainly not the case that they have been unnecessary. Both the new *Collegiate* and the *COD* have *graffito* as head-word without mentioning that *graffiti* is usual as an invariable non-count noun.

Reviewing these handsome new volumes and comparing them with their predecessors of a century ago (and more), one is in fact struck more by the high quality of the old than by the higher quality of the new. Real improvement, real progress there has been: but it has been largely peripheral, and numerous central problems remain virtually untouched. What is a 'word' – or at any rate what should constitute the lexical entry item? (Should *bat an eye-lid* be one entry or three or four? Since *Lombard Street* is in *COD*, why not *Charing Cross Road*?) What are the conditions under which definition slides between ostensive, synonymic, analytic and implicative? What options are open in developing a special metalanguage for expressing definitions? Is Paul Imbs making better use of modern semantic theory in his *Trésor* (Volume I, 1972) than lexicographers in the English-speaking countries? Is it best to order the meanings of poly-semous items historically (the Webster principle), on the basis of currency frequency (Barnhart and Sykes), or in terms of semantic explanation?

Note that the historical principle can give precedence to archaic senses (as with *sad* in *Chambers*). Webster (unabridged and *Eighth Collegiate* alike) give the noun *pipe* its musical sense first, and even the 'two hogsheads' sense precedes the pipe-smoker's pipe; yet, tacitly admitting that there is something unsatisfactory about this, the unabridged opens the entry with a picture of the tobacco pipe. And though Dr Sykes begins with the general tubular sense (which probably well accords with his frequency principle as it certainly would with a semantic principle), he actually interposes not only the musical sense but a specifically labelled archaic sense ('voice, esp. in singing') before we get to parson's pleasure. Nor, of course, if we were to take the frequency principle seriously (as apparently Dr Sykes does not), have we any idea how best to establish frequency: there must be many types of discourse in which the commonest sense of *ticket* is 'summons for a parking offence'.

The foregoing by no means exhausts the basic problems which one would like to see tackled by an advanced lexicological theory. Even when the nature of lexical items is satisfactorily understood, is an alphabetic organization of them the most revealing one? Is it even the most useful for ordinary users?

The only serious breakthrough in this respect takes us back to Bloomsbury again – and is hardly recent. Peter Mark Roget was born nearly 200 years ago and his association with Jeremy Bentham dates from the early years of the nineteenth century. Yet his semantic presentation of the lexicon has remained the only serious contender with the traditional alphabetic one. Now Mairé Kay of the Merriam staff has produced a very interesting combination of the Roget insights with the convenience of the alphabetic dictionary, the *Collegiate Thesaurus* (1976). It is the kind of work whose success can be judged only after prolonged use, but first reactions are on the whole pleasing. Trying to imagine how I would arrive at *collusion* (if this was the *mot juste* at the tip of my tongue but refusing to get further), I found a number of plausible routes quite easily (via *plot*, for example). On the other hand, starting from the notions 'rather off-handed', 'just for form's sake', 'a bit half-hearted', I found no easy way to end up with the required *perfunctory*.

Nor, imagining myself wanting to write to a doctor or government health department and needing the technical or merely 'polite' words or periphrases for intimate physical matters (surely a fairly common need?), could I seem to get any help at all. In other words, there is nothing like an 'inside-out' match between the two eponymous companion volumes, the *Collegiate Thesaurus* and the *Collegiate Dictionary*. Still less can we expect to solve such problems with the much shorter *Reverse Dictionary* of T. M. Bernstein, where the idea is to have meaning paraphrases arranged in alphabetical order and then be given the word that corresponds: e.g. 'small sum of money: PITTANCE'. Here you must start from 'small'; there is no lead under 'money'.

Even with more serious and exhaustive attempts, such as the new Merriam *Thesaurus*, it is clear that we have a long way to go in semantic analysis before real progress can be made. At present, a thesaurus can be only as good as the conventional dictionary resource on which it is based, since its semantic diffusion can scarcely be expected to go beyond the ways by which the meanings of all the words concerned are specified in traditional dictionaries. But there is a chicken-and-egg problem here: dictionary definition itself is in need of overhauling through the very insights that the semantically organized thesaurus approach can supply.

A single example will suffice to show that neither dictionary nor thesaurus as currently devised can reflect the lexical sensibilities inherent in even the most ordinary user's awareness of his language. The participle *damaging* has acquired an abstract sense as an adjective, something like 'hurtful to reputation,' which is not particularly recent but which is difficult if not impossible to extract from the latest Websters or *Chambers* (though *COD* pinpoints it excellently under the verb *damage*). But in addition to this modern sense, *damaging* has a modern collocative tone, a *schadenfroh* tinge, such that I am unlikely to refer to 'a damaging review' of one of my own books. Clearly, this aspect of the *mot juste* would be of great relevance to a thesaurus-user, but he will search in vain. Nor, given the constraints of present lexicographic method, can he expect confirmation of suspected tone by consulting the dictionary entry for such a word.

This in itself is a small point, but it is symptomatic of the way the lexicographer's needle seems to have got stuck. The man who 'busies himself in . . . detailing the signification of words', has never of course needed to be merely a 'harmless drudge' ('I give this as it stands in Johnson,' says R. G. Latham – also symptomatically – in his 'new' edition of 1866). But equally one would not necessarily become a mischievous playboy by engaging in some exciting hypotheses and challenging the largely implicit theories on the nature of words and meanings. Perhaps we shall get genuinely new developments only when universities show more interest in lexicology, undertake serious research in it, and develop some teachable approaches to lexicological theory.

8 Public Words

There is a path in the rather dense forest of linguistics that respectable academics have been rather shy of treading in the past 50 years. This has not been so much because of the briars and potholes as because they have not liked the direction in which it was heading, they have not liked the footprints they could recognize, and above all, perhaps, because they have preferred to follow in the wake of contemporary trail-blazers claiming they were off to somewhere new. Not that the track signposted 'Towards a Better Language' has been deserted: far from it. Yet another reason for its unattractiveness to the fastidious professional has been that it has been tramped enthusiastically by a stream of people whom he has seen less as explorers than as amateur do-gooding missionaries – with a pretty divided sense of mission at that.

Most numerous have been those with the relatively limited goal of making a 'better language' of the one we've got: creating *le bon usage* by restoration and regulation (often, as this example hints, through some such august body as the Académie Française). In the English-speaking countries, they have been especially active from the eighteenth-century Bishop Lowth in England, Richard Grant White in the America of a century later, to Fowler and his successors in our own time. Many of them found they were 'doing *well* by doing good', as Tom Lehrer puts it in another connection, and the popular profitability of Emily Post linguistics has been another (though surely minor) reason for despising it in academic circles.

A more select party has been less concerned with elegance and correctness than with fundamental problems of communicating by means of any among the Babel of natural tongues around us. These

Note: This chapter first appeared as a review of *Language – The Loaded Weapon* by Dwight Bolinger, published in *The London Review of Books* 3(3), February 1981.

languages were hard for other peoples to learn, they were encrusted with treacherous metaphors that concealed the true meaning, and they were ideal weapons for deception in the hands of the unscrupulous. Bentham picked up the trail, following the footsteps, not of Lowth, but of an earlier bishop, John Wilkins, as well as those of Leibniz. That thinking could be influenced and twisted by language concerned Bentham's contemporary Von Humboldt, and an 'academic' line proceeds to the work of Sapir and Whorf in the first half of the twentieth century. A more 'therapeutic' line was developed by such men as Korzybski and Ogden, the former promoting a linguistic hygiene called 'General Semantics' (designed to catch out the knaves), the latter a watery form of universal language, 'Basic English' (in which knavery was supposed to be impossible).

The footprints we miss include those of Whitney, Sweet, De Saussure, Trubetzkoy, Jakobson, Bloomfield, Martinet, Firth, Bloch and Chomsky. And it is not merely that mainline linguists have been busy on trails of their own: it is the fact that the main line has been heading in a direction that seems totally the reverse of the path I have been discussing. The concern of the orthodox linguists has been to examine the human language faculty as it actually appears to operate: to accept it as it is and try to understand its rules and mechanism. Such popular versions of the mainstream as there have been (not all that popular, in fact, and wildly misunderstood) have tended to take an anti-therapeutical stance, encouraging people to use their natural linguistic gifts naturally and to feel confidence in them. All dialects are equal in the sight of the linguistic lords (even though most of them chance to speak in hieratic accents remote from the demotic they praise), and the language of the Harlem black is 'purer' than anything you hear in the Chase Manhattan, where nervous forelock-tugging has mixed a clerk's natural English with things (s)he's plucked from higher up the social tree. Some of the more enthusiastic byproducts of this orthodoxy have reaped a bad press for what is seen to be a vulgar, anti-clerisy permissiveness – not surprisingly, when we recall that Bob Hall's book attempting to popularize orthodox linguistics was entitled *Leave your Language Alone*.

What we have lacked is anyone on the therapeutic path who has seriously studied the implications of descriptive linguistic work. Even a scholar as polymathic as Ogden had for Bloomfield and Firth a contempt that was the harder to shake for the little he would read of their work. But equally, precious few among academic linguists have bothered to concern themselves with the goals of those like Ogden who sought to liberate people from their subjection to the hiding persuaders, or of those like Fowler who sought to cultivate a more widely-spread taste for well-formed speech and writing.

Among the previous few, Dwight Bolinger has made contributions that are especially precious. An immense body of solid descriptive research (primarily in English and Spanish, and always marked by sharpness of insight) puts him firmly in the camp of academic linguists. But he has never been unconcerned about the social relevance of linguistics, and increasingly since his retirement – perhaps, more significantly, since his removal from Harvard to California – he has been drawn into the controversies over linguistic minorities, 'sexism' and other current issues. In 1975, his brilliant *Aspects of Language* came out in a second edition twice the length of the first. The additions, such as a valuable chapter on 'Language and the Public Interest', not merely reflected the fresh explorations of the preceding decade but a wanderlust (or lust for wonder) stimulated by the oldest mysteries.

His new book is precisely devoted to language and the public interest and seeks to interest a wide public. Confident in the unshakable respect of his peers, he can engage himself in issues like the jargon of psychobabble or the tautology of 'the reason is because', without giving the impression of a dowager on an afternoon's charitable slumming. He can sympathetically explore Korzybski's General Semantics without the fear of being thought to have fallen for its exaggerated and misleading claims. He can frankly enforce the goals of therapy without losing sight of (or seeming to lose interest in) the goals of theory. With Jeremy Bentham explicitly in mind, he exposes the way in which language is used to deflect attention from the 'product' to the 'package'. The chapter concerned bears as its title the reassuring words of a chocolate manufacturer: 'We reduced the size because we didn't want to increase the price.'

From so gentle a man, the loaded gun image is perhaps something of a surprise. But it certainly isn't just a gimmick for the cover: it recurs insistently throughout the book ('Loaded language, like loaded firearms, can be hidden where least suspected'), and it is a measure of just how seriously Bolinger takes our plight at the receiving end of linguistic sniping, whether from the sharpshooters in advertising and politics or from the dumdum bullets of the shamans, knocking the life out of language they claim to 'defend from corruption'.

He is rightly hard on this sort of terrorism – at any rate as practised in America: he is transatlantically courteous to what he sees in Britain as 'such respected scholar-shamans as H. W. Fowler and Sir Ernest Gowers'. The 'American species' are to be exposed for their élitism, their antipathy to minorities, their horror of change, and (of course) their gross inconsistency, itself born of ignorance and prejudice. But Bolinger just as rightly acknowledges and respects the ordinary person's concern for standards and his demand for guidance from the experts, well aware that 'shamanite values are those of a majority of writers, critics, editors and other members of the literary community.' So he devotes one of his concluding chapters to an all too rare attempt by an academic linguist to show how much better guidance could come from academic linguists (if only they would take the trouble) than from the blinkered amateurs to whom virtually alone the public can at present turn.

If they have been disinclined to worry about correct usage, on the one hand, or covert deception, on the other, most orthodox linguists have been even more reluctant to get involved in linguistic engineering. Languages are in a constant process of natural change, but deliberate attempts to change them are at best futile, at worst gravely damaging to the society concerned. But Bolinger (and increasing numbers of others) would deny that it is futile, and would point to the limited success of 'language-planning' exercises in a wide range of countries, from Israel to Indonesia. And Bolinger is more willing than most to see that the damage to society is likely to be rather greater in failing to make deliberate linguistic change.

One chapter is devoted to 'A case in point: sexism', where the linguistic indignities to which women have been subjected are compared to the traditional 'innocent merriment of racial slurs', as in 'Eenie-meenie-miney-mo'. Reflecting upon expressions like *black-hearted*, James Baldwin wrote recently that 'for a black writer in this country to be born into the English language is to realise that the assumptions on which the language operates are his enemy.' So, admits Bolinger, are corresponding assumptions the enemy of women. He sees women's libbers, not as sour misandrous (perhaps amandrous) trouble-makers, kicking against the pricks, but as valued allies in making language and society alike more sensitive and responsive. However, in reviewing the pressures of the past decade that have yielded such modest alleviation as *Ms* and *(chair)person*, he also admits that changes in linguistic response can often merely disguise, not remove, the assumptions. He would have seen further evidence of how hard it is to unload 'the gun of sex-biased language' in a London classified advertisement a couple of weeks ago: 'Salesperson wanted, to work with two other ladies.'

9 An Adjunct to Ourself

A natural enough title for an essay on Eric Partridge, when this is precisely what many of us felt we had lost on his death. In almost any aspect of humane letters – literature, languages, book-craft, and of course word-study – he not only had a staggeringly wide knowledge: he had a limitless capacity for sharing it. No query went unanswered. Almost by return of post, always in his own elegant hand, and usually on a tightly packed self-sealing letter-card, came the information we sought, together with references to where more could be obtained. For the hundreds of correspondents who had the good fortune to enjoy his friendship, decade after decade, he became indeed an indispensable adjunct to themselves in their research and writing.

But to Eric himself my title would of course have called up primarily its source in *Love's Labour's Lost* (and the title of the play itself would be a fitting epitaph):

> Learning is but an adjunct of ourself
> And where we are our learning likewise is.

And this would naturally have turned his thoughts to the British Museum – I doubt whether he ever came to speak of the 'British Library'. If, as was claimed by Tze-sze, the grandson of Confucius, merely to be fond of learning is to be near to knowledge, few men ever edged themselves nearer. He was, indeed, fond enough of learning to make it his daily practice not merely to get 'near' but to put himself right in the centre of one of the world's chief repositories of learning. 'Oh no, madam,' a not altogether pleased American scholar was told. 'You can't occupy K1: Mr Partridge will be coming in a few minutes and that is *his* seat.' And so it was – year in, year

Note: This chapter first appeared in *Eric Partridge in His Own Words*, edited by David Crystal (1980).

out. He made the BM his second home, with a ticket first issued in November 1923 and regularly renewed (with only a short war-time break while he was serving in the RAF) for well over half a century. No scholar made more exiguous demands on the staff but none was better known to them, and each Christmas he acknowledged his modest debt with a cheque, tentatively suggesting 'chocolates for the girls and some Embassy Panatellas for the men . . . to the limit of what the traffic will bear.'*

And for Partridge what the traffic could bear was never very much. Though the scores of friends he generously hosted at the Savile were given no reason to suspect it, he remained a man of acutely slender means. ('Business, you know, may bring money, but friendship hardly ever does,' Jane Austen tells us in *Emma*, and Partridge's instincts were unshakeably set on friendship.) In a period when almost all others engaged in writing on language had the financial security of an academic post behind them, with any royalties merely easing the mortgage a bit, Partridge lived for the major part of his fourscore years and five on royalties alone. The brief exceptions are revealing: a couple of years in the twenties as a university teacher and four running his own small publishing business until the 1931 slump put him out of business. They are revealing because they highlight the extent to which Partridge's strengths were limited: he was at his best with a pen in his hand, with none of the responsibilities of administering a business or of teaching students. In truth, although he was a delightful conversationalist, he froze into calamitously dull immobility of mind when he went before a microphone (he broadcast occasionally) or a lectern (he was invited to do so less and less frequently).

Unfortunately, this did not merely constitute an incidental limitation: it actually contributed to a far more serious and more central one. His dependence on royalties diverted his attentions all too often from the historical study of slang (his forte, as well as his prime interest from about 1930). If he had been able to get into the school market with one widely used text-book, he would have had a financial cushion on which his serious interests could have reclined. But this he never achieved, and he came to depend on the layman's interest in the byways of language (widespread enough, but not fortune-making) and the layman's concern for 'good usage' (already

*I am indebted for this charming detail to Mr J. A. Marks of the British Library.

pretty well catered for by Fowler, not to mention other 'readers over your shoulder' like A. P. Herbert). This meant not just a diversion of his interest but a dilution of them. Let me give one example, about which I have something of a bad conscience because I chided Partridge over it in my naïvety, before I had come to realize the economic pressures on him.

After his fairly successful attempt to up-stage Fowler with *Usage and Abusage* (New York 1942, London 1947), he wrote *Chamber of Horrors* for the André Deutsch Language Library series of which he was founder and general editor. But he published it under the name 'Vigilans'. In the Preface, 'Vigilans' warmly thanks Partridge: to him 'I owe a special debt. He has encouraged and helped me in the search for jargon . . . and written an Introduction.' And in the said Introduction, nine pages long and of course signed by Partridge, he in turn (page 14) commends the work of 'Vigilans'.

This seemed more than a literary jest, as he represented it to Ivor Brown (the dedicatee: 'Gracious Guardian of English') as well as to me and other friends. Coming so soon after *Usage and Abusage* (and containing in large measure material already in that book), it would have looked a bit repetitious to have the *Chamber of Horrors* in his own name – in his own series. But the 'Vigilans' device not only relieved its author of this embarrassment but enabled him to quote himself glowingly on page after page, with the name of Partridge linked with Fowler, Gowers, Alan Herbert and Ifor Evans, whose handbooks were held up along with Partridge's as the authorities on good usage – as well as being rifled for supportive quotations. Thus on *priority* (page 102), 'Vigilans' writes: 'All loyal to the cause of good English would do well to heed the verdict expressed in Eric Partridge's *Usage and Abusage.*' On page 124 we find no fewer than three such puffs; for example, 'I recommend all diligent inquirers to go to both "Fowler" and "Partridge" '.

If financial pressures led him to dilution and self-advertisement, it diverted him also to write – engagingly enough – ephemera like *Comic Alphabets* and *The 'Shaggy Dog' Story*, as well as layman's guides to such diverse matters as onomastics and punctuation (*You Have a Point There* – Partridge had a flair for titles). And his nose for what should sell produced *Shakespeare's Bawdy* – which, if he could have taken more time and space, his nose for bawdy could have made so very much better.

Whether everything he wrote could have been much better is hard to say. It is perhaps significant that even his most serious work was more highly praised by the literary than the philological establishment. His etymologies (*Origins*, 1958) were based on literary scholarship and intuitive judgement more than on philological theory. In fact, he seemed to distrust theory and certainly ignored most theoretical adventures from Bloomfield and the Prague School onwards. It was characteristic that he should have spent his last years on a dictionary of catchphrases without in the least being troubled by the vagueness of the term itself: 'Friends – and others – have often asked me, "What the devil *is* a catch phrase?" I don't know' (Introduction). Yet in his knowledge he was profound and in his reading omnivorous (as the present memorial volume illustrates clearly enough). It was on these grounds – together with his endlessly patient kindness – that he was so invaluable 'an adjunct to ourself'. He helped others of like mind. The encouragement he gave to scores of young writers in – or at the fringe of – language studies put many of them on the first rungs of the career ladder, as well as introducing them to an exciting circle of friends such as Christopher Fry, Gilbert Harding and Robert Morley.

It is difficult and perhaps too soon to make a proper assessment of the impact that this prolific scholar has had: still more difficult to assess the impact he will have in the future. Few libraries are without at least some of his books, yet he is little read – and is least read (and perhaps always has been) by those most concerned with the direction of language studies. Nonetheless, and gloomy as are the implications of this, there seem to be three areas in which one can speak of positive influence.

First, there is his standing among those whose job involves writing: I don't mean poets, novelists, dramatists (though I don't exclude them either) so much as civil servants, solicitors, administrators, secretaries. For such people (who are arguably the most vulnerable to critics of their usage and style), 'Partridge' became something of a household word in the same category as 'Fowler', though never with the same aura of authority or anything like the same ubiquity. His staying-power as such a household word is doubtful, but I am confident that his many writings on usage will continue (along with comparable contributions by Fowler, A. P. Herbert, Ivor Brown, Ernest Gowers and Bruce Fraser) to have a pervasive if perhaps anonymous influence in alerting the writing public to the need for clarity and the avoidance of pomposity.

Secondly, there is the stimulus he gave to writings upon language, especially on English, and especially for students and the lay public. This stimulus he exercised above all through the books he edited for André Deutsch, and while some of the volumes have been of so low a standard as to risk damaging the series as a whole, there is little question that the Language Library has had (and under its new direction will increasingly have) a beneficial effect in extending a knowledge of language studies. Indeed, it is chiefly by this means that Partridge has been able to have some influence within universities and other institutions of higher education.

But in my view it is in the third area that he will have a really lasting impact: his lexicographic work, and especially that on slang (even his etymological dictionary, *Origins*, is at its best with slang and tabu).

Given the quite severe limitations self-imposed by Murray and his colleagues, the great *OED* left the field of argot, slang, colloquialism wide open – and much in need of care and attention. Partridge gave it both. Though he regrettably lacked the means to emulate Murray in subjecting primary sources to detailed study, he did a very useful job in collating the evidence presented in numerous collections of slang words, liberally adding material from his own eclectic reading and – for the present century – from his own memory. The results (*A Dictionary of Slang and Unconventional English*, 1937, with its pre- and post-war supplements) lack the magisterial scholarship, meticulous authentication, and consistency of presentation that give us confidence in the *OED*, but Partridge's work is the best we are likely to have for a long time. And as a one-man product, it is deeply impressive. The three or four column-inches on *pross* and its derivatives are a good illustration.

One of the strong points of the *Dictionary* is the attention paid to phrasal colloquialisms such as 'right as ninepence', and in a sense Partridge's last major work, *A Dictionary of Catch Phrases* (1977), can be seen as a final supplement (after forty years) to the *Dictionary of Slang*. To the *Catch Phrases* in turn there was to be a supplement, and in one of his last letters to me (8 March 1979), Partridge resolutely maintained his intention of continuing with this (he had already got to 'T'), though now weak and confined to a Devon nursing home. While resenting his grievously reduced capacity and the indignities imposed by his ageing body, he could find the irony to blame only himself for his condition ('far too much hard work, over far too long a period') and even to take grim pleasure in permuting a catch phrase he might well have put in his collection: 'one need not grin; it is enough to be obliged to bear it.' *The Dictionary of Catch Phrases* is marred by some dilution and prolixity: for example, in comparing two obviously similar phrases (page 197), he says that the first 'is a naval lower-deck variant' of the second, 'than which it is felt to be slightly less coarse, slightly less offensive, and slightly more polite'. And there is the rather too frequent practice of tantalizingly omitting textual support. Thus *don't want to know* is asserted to originate in British jails of the present century – perhaps correctly, but evidence would have been welcome from the one man who was likely to have some. The dictionary is none the less invaluable, if only (again) because we cannot realistically expect to have anything better in the foreseeable future.

At the same time, it is invaluable also in providing a late demonstration of Partridge's wide-ranging interests and the sheer delight he took in the byways of language. There is an article, for example, on 'Oh, Mother, is it worth it?'. Oh, Eric, it was.

10 Grammatical and Pragmatic Aspects of Countability

At the interface of grammar and pragmatics, we find several groups of entity, for reference to which the simple polarities at our disposal (notably singular and plural, count and non-count) are less than wholly accommodating.[1] There is for instance the evidence of the count/non-count homophones such that, beside the neat formal separation of *a loaf* and *some bread* or semantic separation of *a glass* and *some glass*, we have *a cake* and *some cake* where little more than speaker's point of view need be involved. There are the collectives which with obligatory singular determiners can have singular or plural verb concord, and a pronominal reference with choice of both number and personal/non-personal contrast: *this family (company, committee . . .) which/who is/are. . . it/they. . . .* There are the invariably plural nouns, for example the summation plurals (Quirk *et al.* 1972, 4.54) referring to 'composite objects' (Jespersen 1949, II.4.7), uneasily combining a broadly plural grammar with a broadly singular meaning, and involving in some cases homophony with other noun groups, as in *these glasses are bifocal*.

With these and some other groups of anomalies, the phenomena are reasonably well described, with fairly clear limits of variation meeting reasonably well established conditions of acceptability. My concern in this chapter is with a small set of nouns for which these conditions do not hold.

Among nouns normally treated as non-count, in so far as grammar reflects our perception in this respect, there is a group comprising both 'concrete' and 'abstract' nouns which collocate with verbs of (dis)assembly in a way implying countability:

Note: This chapter first appeared in *Die Neueren Sprachen* 77 (1978).
[1]This article proceeds from ongoing research in the Survey of English Usage, financed in part with the help of the Leverhulme Trust Fund.

> he gathered (assembled, scattered, dispersed . . .) a little money (news, information, material . . .)

Contrast:

> *he gathered (assembled, scattered, dispersed . . .) a little butter (research, safety . . .)

The set is not perfectly homogeneous in this respect (*he scattered/*dispersed a little bread*), but appears in general to give little trouble to the native speaker except for a number of items that might be regarded as a distinct subgroup, comprising chiefly *data*, *(mass-)media, paraphernalia, regalia. .*

These, it will be noted, are 'foreign plurals', but while this fact is by no means irrelevant, the problems attending these nouns must be sharply distinguished from the commonplace and relatively trivial difficulties among people (generally – but by no means exclusively[2] – of low educational level) who are liable to use *phenomena* or *criteria* as singulars. In such cases, there seems to be a firmly apprehended categorization of the nouns as countable, and the tendency in question is merely to treat them as number-invariant like *sheep*: *this one criteria is enough for me; there were three strange phenomena*. With *strata*, the position is more complicated since while countability firmly obtains (*three strata of rock/society*) the strata themselves may pragmatically entail perception as collectives. Thus with the 'strata' of society, any of which may comprise millions of people, we need not be surprised to find sociologists using the form with the grammatical and semantic properties of *group*: *this strata of society tends/tend to . . . .*

With the *data* set (despite Juul 1975,14, who includes *data* in his syncretism class along with *sheep* etc.), we have a rather different (and more interesting) problem. There is a far more persistent tendency to use singular determiners, verb concord and pronominal reference with these items, despite awareness (uneasy awareness, as is commonly made explicit) on the part of the educated that they are 'strictly' (Latin) plurals.[3] Such awareness is firmly endorsed by the

---

[2] A reviewer in *Language* (52 (1976), 997) comments acidly on the usage in a book by Derek Bickerton, published by the Cambridge University Press: '*Data* is variously mass and plural count; phenomena is singular.'

[3] It is doubtful whether educational status (see footnote 2) or language 'variety' (e.g. formal *v.* informal) is as significant a factor in concord variation as the clash between pragmatics and the straitjacket of a two-term number contrast. But cf. Pound 1919, Juul 1975, 24*f*, 180, 217*f*, and perhaps especially Mittins *et al.*1970, 32*ff*.

leading dictionaries. Neither the *Oxford Dictionary* (1933) nor *Webster* (1971) says anything under the entry *data* except that this is the plural of *datum*, and it is under the latter that the uses of *data* are presented; so too the *Oxford Supplement* (1972). As for *media*, *Webster* (1971) makes no separate entry for the 'communications' sense, treating it only as a subsection of one of the 13 meanings of *medium*. On the other hand, the *Oxford Supplement* (1976), in contrast to its treatment of *data*, has a distinct entry for *media* in which all relevant citations are presented.

Singular usage is mentioned in *Webster* (*media* 'sometimes'[4], *data* 'often', but without further comment), and is amply illustrated in the *Oxford Supplement*: in the case of *data* without comment, though with *media* and *mass media* there are explicit notes that this is 'erroneous'. But erroneous or not, it should be clear that such singular construction is on a very different acceptability footing from expressions like *this is a useful criteria*. For one thing, it is far more frequent; for another, it occurs in the writing (as well as the speech) of those who would never use *one criteria*; for yet another, it is susceptible of explicit defence by those who find it natural. The *Oxford Supplement* has a 1965 citation: '*data* is now accepted as a singular collective noun' (J. Allan, *Speaking of Computers*, 5).

Speaking of linguistics, however, it will not quite do to characterize *data* as a 'collective noun'. It is true that, like normal collectives such as *family, herd, jury*, we have with *data* a choice of verb concord (*the gang was/were, the data was/were*) and of reference pronoun (*the family . . . it/they; the data . . . it/they; The family/the data speak(s) for itself/themselves*). But whereas the plurality aspect of collectives cannot be reflected in the choice of determiners (*this/that family/jury/herd/class, *these/those family . . .*), with *data* it can: *this/these/that/those data*. Again, where collectives usually share quantification properties only with count nouns (*many of the gang/committee, *much of the gang/committee*), *data* can be used with non-count and plural count quantifiers alike: *much/many of the data*.

In these latter respects, *media* tends to be used rather more like collectives than does *data*, but there is one significant respect in which *media* and *data* are brought together in sharp contrast to

---

[4]Also *paraphernalia*, but not *regalia* which indeed is treated only under the 'singular' trisyllabic head word *regale*.

normal count nouns, whether collectives or not. They can be count nouns in respect only of general quantifiers (*some, many* etc.) and not of cardinal numerals: **fourteen data, *three media*. In this connection, it is striking that, despite the unequivocal dictionary claim that they are the plurals of *datum* and *medium* (which is true enough up to a point), we cannot normally use *datum* and *medium* as the singulars of these words without conspicuous pedantry or facetiousness: *if I could add to my data another datum like that; we have an excess of mass media already and to launch a new medium would be to court bankruptcy*. Cardinal countability can be imposed only with the device of phrasal partitives: *N item(s) of data, N section(s) of the media, one part of her regalia, a dozen pieces of paraphernalia*. This last fact, together with the constraint on selecting partitives that are more or less item-specific, provides a clue as to why a class of 'aggregate' nouns should exist, quite sharply distinct (as can be seen in the summary provided by the diagram) from other noun classes.

Some noun types in relation to selected grammatical features

		Sing. verb	Pl. verb	*this*	*these*	*many of*	*much of*	Card. num.
count	non-collective (*fingers*)	−	+	−	+	+	−	+
	collective (*family*)	+	+	+	−	+	−	−
pluralia	tantum (*earnings*)	−	+	−	+	−	+	−
aggregate'	(*data*)	+	+	+	+	+	+	−
non-count	(*butter*)	+	−	+	−	−	+	−

The grammar of the count noun is admirably equipped for reference to entities which are individually identifiable and which when grouped both preserve this individuality and are perceived as having an effective homogeneity. *Another* child joins a group of *eleven children* and there are then *twelve children*: each is 'regarded as single and complete in itself, an individual or unit belonging to a class of similar objects', as Christophersen puts it (1939,26); cf also Jespersen (1949,II.4.11).

At the other extreme, we have entities in respect of which countability is pragmatically inconceivable (*butter*, *leisure*) or pragmatically irrelevant (*oats*, *rice*). Grammar is adjusted to our perception in a rather more ad hoc way. We have a range of quantifiers of the non-discrete, 'less/more' type and partitives semantically appropriate to the way in which the entities are apportioned: a pat of butter, a shovelful (or truckload) of earth, a pound of oats, a litre of water. And we achieve the necessary disengagement from the number system only by neutralization of the singular/plural contrast: the singular or plural deixis and concord forms cannot themselves be avoided, however 'alien' (Christophersen, *ibid*) they are to items of this kind. Thus *leisure* is construed with singular and *oats* with plural. The extent to which grammatical categories can be harmonized with such entities when mediated through the concept of 'continuity' and 'discontinuity' (as suggested particularly by the glossematicians) is usefully discussed in Sten 1949.

But of course no-one questions the unease with which we are ultimately faced by such binary choices. *Are you on the pill?* and *man tends to congregate in cities* illustrate noun phrases outside the singular/plural contrast as much as do *butter* and *oats*, even though *congregate* semantically entails plural as much as *tends* grammatically entails singular. We can have semantically well formed sentences which, through the lack of grammatically well formed exponents, cannot properly be expressed: *neither you nor I ?is/are/am right.* The summation plurals display some arbitrariness in their (largely) binary countability: *my best pair of trousers* = *my best trousers*, but *my two best pairs of trousers* ≠ **my two best trousers*. Indeed, viewed pragmatically they are arbitrary in their very existence: shirts have two 'arms' as inalienably as trousers have two 'legs'; a bra (or, with its two sides, a coin) is no less inherently bipartite than a pair of spectacles. In his discussion of analogous mismatches between perceived reality and grammatical categories, Bolinger (1969,38) has shown that the noun *weather* stoutly 'resists the tests that usually identify Mass and Count.' Cf also Sørensen (1958, 135) on such noun phrases as *a Gainsborough*. Nor should we ignore the evidence provided by the common reallocation of items with the passage of time: *pea(s)* in relation to earlier *pease*; the eighteenth-century controversy over *means* and *a mean*; the history of *die, dies, dice* – curiously enough, cognate with *data*.[5]

Certainly, the *data* group confronts us with a striking instance of phenomena for which sharp separation into count and non-count is inevitably resisted. Their referents are clearly apprehended as aggregates and yet equally clearly comprise components that are difficult to perceive as individual or homogeneous. The media consist of newspapers, press agencies, radio organizations and other disparate elements. Data likewise must be an aggregation of facts, reports, statistics, impressions, so that a kind of plurality is essential for apprehension of the complex phenomena involved. But it is just as essential in operating with these entities to be able to ignore the component nature of the phenomena and to treat them as having an amalgam operation. As Monsen rightly insists (1976, 109), we are not directly concerned in language with the 'real' nature of such entities: we are concerned only with 'our perception' of them.

This has the effect that when linguistic form forces us unduly to choose too sharply between count and non-count categories for such items as *data*, we can become uncomfortably aware of the inappropriateness. It is better to be able to say *the data may be inadequate* than either *this is not enough data* or *these data are too few*. Despite the insistence of the dictionaries, we may doubt whether a native speaker of English would so readily have used the form *too many technical paraphernalia* which appeared (oddly enough in a discussion of error analysis) in the *Interlanguage Studies Bulletin* (Utrecht 1976, I.336).

Taking *data* as the classic example of this 'aggregate' class, we have in fact the interpenetration of two sets of problems. In the first place, it is formally an exotic plural – a fact of which no person involved with the word in serious study is likely to be unaware and which is insisted upon by dictionaries and the like. In the second place, we have a range of common uses, some of which are fully congruent with a singular/plural contrast: not merely is *datum* a natural singular form for these but for some of them (*Webster* (1971): 'a point . . . with reference to which positions . . . are measured'; *Longman* (1976): 'a starting point') a re-formed plural *datums* is actually the form in common use[6]. With other uses, a

---

[5]Cf. also the reanalysis of several plural count and pluralia tantum nouns in some European languages: e.g. *Keks, Komiks, slams* are singular count in Polish (plural *Keksy, Komiksy, slamsy*).

[6]Cf. the fully established lexical split between *stamen* (count; plural *stamens*) and *stamina* (non-count).

number contrast is irrelevant to the perceived pragmatic facts, and we get the concord problems that frequently arise when there is conflict between form and meaning (cf. Strang 1966, e.g. in relation to *means*, 81).

A glance at the occurrence of *data* in the work of Noam Chomsky may be of some interest for several reasons. First, he is a scholar for whom the collection and use of data as commonly practised in the physical and behavioural sciences have had little interest; the word *data* is not therefore frequently or insistently used in his writing and is less likely than with some scholars to settle into a grammatical cliché of regularized concord practice. Secondly, we have good longitudinal textual evidence (1955 to the present), with a range of material both published and unpublished that enables us to offset the standardizing effect of the printing establishment and thus to assess Chomsky's own practice. Thirdly, he is a man well-known for intellectual independence and hence unlikely to feel slavishly responsive to sociolinguistic normative pressures. We might there-fore expect his usage to be especially determined by solely semantic and pragmatic factors. (But see footnote 7 below.)

The word is used by Chomsky in one of two principal ways: on the one hand, the evidence or material which the linguist sets out to explain; on the other hand, the language experience to which the learner is exposed in the acquisition process. It will be noticed that in neither case, from a pragmatic viewpoint, is countability either excluded or enjoined: for both uses, fully count or fully non-count paraphrases (*facts, experience, phenomena, material*) can and do occur. And there is little evidence that Chomsky connects one of these senses with countability any more than the other.

Throughout the entire span of his writings we find instances of *data* with singular determiners and verb concord and with quan-tifiers congruent with the perception of data as an agglomerate. Thus 'we can demonstrate that the data does have the prescribed form', 'this data', 'no serious data is available', 'the data has been col-lected' (typescript version of *The Logical Structure of Linguistic Theory* (1955), I-21, IV-161, IV-3*fn*, VII-1*fn*). Similar instances occur in *Word* 17 (1961), 219, 225; *Proceedings of the Ninth International Congress of Linguists* (1964), 924, 926, 938, 941, 966 (e.g. 'much of the data that is to be explained'); *Current Issues in Linguistic Theory* (1964), 29, 31, 59; *Cartesian Linguistics* (1966), 'the data itself', 65; *Reflections on Language* (1975), 'operating on that data', 15; the typescript 'On *Wh*-Movement' (1976), footnote 31.

Yet equally throughout the period there is analogous (and rather more) linguistic evidence of data being perceived as a plurality of phenomena. Indeed, in the first of the works cited above, the typescript of 1955, we get some uses of the singular *datum* as in I-1*fn*: 'not every recorded observation need be accepted as a datum', with the implication that 'data' would be a set of such observations, sightings, occurrences. In the *Word* article of 1961 there are more instances of *data* with overt plural grammar than there are with singular (219, 223, 227), and at one point there is the remark, 'it is here that the data cannot be enumerated' (222), which clearly entails the existence also of *numerable* data. In 'The Logical Basis of Linguistic Theory' (1964), while 'singular' usage is overwhelmingly predominant, there is at least one 'plural' occurrence: 'data of this sort are . . . what constitute . . .' (939). Again, in *Current Issues* (1964), beside a majority of singulars, we find a plural on p.56. By contrast, in *Aspects of the Theory of Syntax* (1965), in which singular concord is rare, there are numerous instances of the plural being used (e.g. 26, 27, 32, 33ff, 193, 202, 207), including several striking pronominal references with *they*. But beside the use of such words as 'scattered', congruent enough with countables, we find occasional expressions suggesting non-count agglomeration: 'a complex of data that differentiates . . .' (26), 'enormous mass of . . . data' (20), 'primary linguistic data *D* constitutes a sample' (209).

We would in fact be rash to suppose that the growing preponderance of 'plural' usage in his more recent writings (e.g. *Reflections*, 28, 154, 231, 245f) points to Chomsky's increased perception of data as comprising separable and numerable phenomena (like 'facts', 'instances', 'arguments') rather than varying amounts and qualities of material ('evidence') to which the grammatical category of number is inapplicable. There are interesting ambiguities, such as on p.39 of the typescript 'On *Wh*-movement': 'If there is a systematic distinction, contrary to the data of (91), (92), then either the analysis is incorrect or there is still another source for clefts.'

The (91) and (92) in question are contrasting sets of synonymous sentences of the form 'Out of spite, I asked them' and 'It was out of spite that I asked them' respectively. These are followed by (93) which shows that a superficially similar pair of sentences are not exactly synonymous. How now are we to read 'contrary to the data of (91), (92)'? On the one hand, we may be invited to look at several facts or instances, each and all of which suggest a possible solution. On the other hand, (91) and (92) may be regarded as comprising a class of evidence, the individual parts of which are irrelevant, indicating a single principle. The whole tenor of Chomskyan linguistic theory, based on overriding principle rather than on conclusions emerging from the sum of individual facts, makes the latter – it seems to me – unquestionably more plausible.[7]

The foregoing 'case study' bears out the claim that items like *data* constitute a special class with its own set of grammatical tolerances. These tolerances, untidy though they seem, correspond in part to the varying pull of linguistic tradition (the implications of 'known' plurality) but more especially to the semantic factors at work as these words are applied to perceived aspects of the non-linguistic world.

To what extent the range of grammatical possibilities in respect of the *data* group is a recent development is not entirely clear. Visser (1970, 62ff) has demonstrated conclusively that – so far as the straightforward collectives are concerned – there has always from OE times existed the freedom to use singular or plural concord according to the 'constructio ad sensum' required by the writer's perception in a given instance. It is even possible, he feels, that the freedom to ignore strictly 'grammatical' concord was greater in earlier times, and it would not be surprising if it diminished following the upsurge of normative purism in the eighteenth century. For the *data* group, the evidence of the *Oxford Dictionary* (1933) citations would suggest that plural concord was more strictly observed at one time than it is now (though the 'singular' with *paraphernalia* has long been common enough), and this would account in part for·the emphasis that dictionaries continue to put on the plural status of these words.

---

[7]If this is so, then we must look for an alternative explanation of the increased grammatical plurality of Chomsky's *data*. Comparison of the 1955 typescript with the printed version of *Logical Structure* (New York: Plenum Press 1975) shows the curious fact that, where the corresponding passages survive, all the noted instances of 'singular' *data* have been 'pluralized'. Thus the three examples quoted above now read: 'the data do have' (p.86), 'these data' (p.152), 'the data have been' (p.227). Since the many major changes in the text are obviously authorial, we have no good reason to suppose that these minor ones have been written in by a pedantic editor.

If in fact we have a genuine decline in plural use, this might be accounted for in several ways. The nature of the entities concerned may in 'real' terms have changed in a direction justifying increased perception as non-count; this seems especially plausible with *data*, since the growth of research in the physical and social sciences (along with computational means of handling material) has led to larger and larger quantities of data being assembled and used. Alternatively the reason may lie in sociolinguistic change: the decline in knowledge of and respect for the classical languages has loosened the association of *-a* with plural (cf. *one criteria*); and the cultivation of a more informal style of language, even in serious scientific writing, has doubtless encouraged the ignoring of 'strictly correct' usage in this as in other respects. But the evidence presented from Chomsky should make us cautious over regarding this as a powerful trend.

References

Bolinger, D. 1969: 'Categories, Features, Attributes.' *Brno Studies in English* **8**, 37–41.

Christophersen, P. 1939: *The Articles*. Copenhagen: Munksgaard.

Jespersen, O. 1949: *A Modern English Grammar*, II (rev. N. Haislund). Copenhagen: Munksgaard.

Juul, A. 1975: *On Concord of Number in Modern English*. Copenhagen: Nova.

Longman Modern English Dictionary (ed. Owen Watson). London: Longman, 1976.

Mittins, W. H., Salu, M., Edminson, M. and Coyne, S. *et al.* 1970: *Attitudes to English Usage*. London: Oxford University Press.

Monsen, T. 1976: *Fragments of a Theory of Countability and Mass in Modern English*. Oslo (mimeo).

Oxford English Dictionary. Oxford: Clarendon Press 1933. *A Supplement* (ed. R. W. Burchfield). Oxford: Clarendon Press, 1972, 1976.

Pound, L. 1919: 'The Pluralization of Latin Loan-Words in Present-Day American Speech.' *The Classical Journal* 15, 163–8.

Quirk, R., Greenbaum, S., Leech, G. and Svartvik, J. 1972: *A Grammar of Contemporary English*. London: Longman.

Sørensen, H. S. 1958: *Word-Classes in Modern English*. Copenhagen: Gad.

Sten, H. 1949: 'Le Nombre grammatical.' *Travaux du Cercle Linguistique de Copenhague* **4**, 47–59.

Strang, B. M. H. 1966: 'Some Features of S-V Concord in Present-Day English.' *English Studies Today* **4**, 73–87.

Visser, F. T. 1970: *An Historical Syntax of the English Language*. Leiden: Brill.

Webster's Third New International Dictionary. Springfield: Merriam, 1971.

11 Focus, Scope, and Lyrical Beginnings

The sense of an ending (cf. Kermode 1966) is well established – whether of an insitution or a man's life or a poem or even a lecture – however much we may be forced by peripeteia to revise our naive ideas (or hopes) of what constitutes fitness of ending in a given case. The sense of a *beginning* is in principle more problematic – since for one thing, of course, by definition nothing can begin without the postulation of an end. Moreover, while we expect to recognize endings (the fall of a·tree, the death of a president, the consummation of sexual love), beginnings are diffident, obscure, literally negligible things. As Shelley put it, though *wingèd* sure enough, seeds first lie cold and low, corpse-like in their grave (or womb), before facing whatever west wind is to be their *preserver* (and, ironically, their destroyer).

So far as discourse is concerned, let us not press our inquiry into the dark wintry period of gestation, still less speculate on the means or instant of conception. I want to direct attention to the moment when the beginning springs into linguistic form. Not, in all conscience, to try and show how (reversing Eliot) our beginnings always know our ends, but rather to explore the strategies we may adopt to show that we have made a beginning. Or rather to *pretend* we have. Because I am particularly interested in our effective awareness that beginnings do not exist: we have only continuations.

Suppose I come into a room where some friends of mine are reading in silence, and I begin: 'John's been fired!' It will be noticed that this has to be said to friends: I cannot thus 'begin' a conversation with strangers. It has to be with people that know who John is, who know about his job, and who are likely to be concerned over the implications of his losing it. This is what I mean by saying that such a

Note: This chapter first appeared in *Language and Style* XI (1978).

'beginning' is really a continuation.

It is arguable that even attempts to begin discourse with complete strangers are continuations, in the sense that we take as our 'starting point' *topics* (cf. Li 1976) (a key word in this connection) known to be conventionally established as common ground in our society:

(1) Do you happen to know what time it is?

rather than, say,

(2) Do you happen to know what time Mr Kosygin leaves for work every morning?

though (2) may in fact be of much greater interest to the inquirer and would certainly better justify the tentative form of his question ('Do you happen to know . . .'). And if we begin not with a question but with a 'statement', it will surely be something like

(3) The weather's turning nasty

rather than

(4) The nearest star is about ten light-years from the earth

though it might be rational to suppose that the stranger's interest would be greater and his knowledge more genuinely increased by (4) than by (3).

But take an instance of a beginning that is somewhat more unexpected than an inquiry about the time or a comment on the weather. Let us imagine someone leaning across in a plane or a train and saying to a stranger:

(5) Excuse me, are you a doctor?

Even this is a continuation, of course. In the first place, he is saying 'Are you one of that class of professionals that in our society we refer to as doctors, meaning medical practitioners?' The seeds of this beginning lie darkly hidden in our common knowledge of the language. A doctor of divinity and a PhD in linguistics would alike reply 'No'. In the second place, whether answering 'No' or 'Yes', the stranger addressed would probably go on to say 'Are you feeling ill?' In other words, this beginning is also a continuation of established norms, of rational expectations based on earlier experience. He would not reply 'No' or 'Yes', settling back into his book, saying to himself, 'Ah, another person who is unable (or able) to guess the occupation of a stranger.'

Yet there is an important sense in which (5) is nearer to being a beginning than if the stranger had been addressed with the question:

(6) Excuse me, are you the doctor?

which sets up quite different and far more immediate implications of continuation by reason of the lightly uttered distinction between the definite and the indefinite article. And here is where I turn from pragmatic, conventional and conceptual consideration of beginnings to the more linguistic aspects.

Consider for a moment the linguistic devices to be observed in one of our most traditional openings of a narrative:

(7) Once upon *a* time, there was *a* princess[1] who lived in *a* big castle.[2] *Her*[1] father[3] filled *it*[2] with well-armed soldiers[4] to guard *his*[3] gold and jewels. One of *these*[4] soldiers fell in love with *the*[1] princess . . .

We see a progression from indefinite (for what is newly introduced: *a princess, a castle, soldiers*) to pronominal and definite for what has to be regarded as now securely established or given (*her, it, his, these soldiers, the princess*). Even the wholly stereotyped 'once upon *a* time' obeys this rule: we could expect the story to go on, 'At *that* time, a soldier wasn't encouraged to fall for a princess', where *that time* would refer back to the period *a time* in which the narrative was located. This is a further indication that our example earlier of a probable opening to a stranger in (3) is not really a beginning. We tacitly agree that *the* weather exists as *a priori* common ground between us.

But there is another device in (7) that is vital to linguistic beginnings: it is the existential formula which allows us to signal newness not just with the indefinite article but by the placement of the noun phrase concerned at the *end* of our opening clause:

There was once a princess

It is obviously important, if we are bringing something new onto our conversational stage, that our listeners can as it were see the curtain going up and get ready to focus their attention. The existential structure does not of course literally make an announcement about existence: it does so in a conventionally figurative way, in order to bring the existence to our listeners' notice. There are various such existential curtain-raiser devices which ensure that the newly introduced item is put at the most striking focal place of the initial clause – the final, climactic, most prominent position:

> There was *a man I knew* who . . .
> I once had *a friend* who . . .
> The other day I was faced with *a real problem*. It . . .
> You remember *old Jim Davidson*? Well, he . . .

It is in this sense that I use *focus* in my title.

We will return to questions of linguistic form presently, but first let me make one obvious but important point: it is our common experience that discourse does not always have such clearly marked beginnings. More often, probably, we are not in on the beginnings at all: we join a conversation that is already in progress. We tune in as best we can, decide what the pronouns refer to, what the implications of definite articles are, try to figure out who is saying what about whom, and – though sometimes getting the wrong end of the stick – do our best to work our way backwards and set up our own construct of what has gone before.

And not just in conversation, of course. Richard DiLello begins *The Longest Cocktail Party* (his 1972 book about the Beatles) with the unidentified speech of two people as follows:

> 'So how did you come to get this job? What were you doing before, and where are you from?'
> 'I don't really like talking about myself –'
> 'Well, look, this book is your idea, not mine. I mean, you've got to say *something*.'

You, I, this job, this book. Who is talking to whom about what? More than a page of this dialogue confronts us before we can establish the identity of even one speaker: the author DiLello himself.

Now, of course, sophisticated fiction has long imitated reality in this respect. While traditional epic clings to a formal beginning,

> Sing, O Goddess, the wrath of Peleus's son (*Iliad*)
> I sing of arms and the man who came from Troy (*Aeneid*)
> We have heard of the power of the Spear-Danes (*Beowulf*)

Sir Philip Sidney tells us that by an alternative strategy 'a Poet thrusteth into the middest' (cf. Kermode 1966, 7), and we can see plenty of examples of this in the work of his contemporary, Shakespeare. Most obviously, one need hardly say, in the drama. Let us imagine attending a performance of *The Tempest* as a completely unknown play. Two men come on to the stage and address each other as follows:

'Boatswain!'

'Here, master. What cheer?'

'Good, speak to the mariners. Fall to it yarely, or we run ourselves
    aground.'

Nothing here to suggest that we are watching a play about Prospero
and his daughter; about Caliban and Ariel. Contrast the traditional
story-opening a couple of centuries later in the Lambs' *Tales from
Shakespeare*, using an existential formula plus indefinites:

> There was a certain island in the sea, the only inhabitants of which were
> an old man, whose name was Prospero, and his daughter Miranda, a
> very beautiful young lady.

But while Sidney's thrusting 'into the middest' is merely 'realistic'
in the drama or the novel, it is of course absolutely *essential* to the
writer of a lyric who denies himself the luxury of space to introduce
his material with the ordered leisure enjoyed by Charles and Mary
Ann Lamb. Only the relatively vacuous limerick can afford an
existential formula: the sonnet, pledged to make a serious point with
a real sense of ending, must forego any sense of beginning. Yet
equally, with only 140 syllables to go from countdown, the
sonneteer is debarred from giving himself the seeming free range in
an ongoing discourse that the dramatist has with several acts ahead
of him, or DiLello with two or three hundred pages. The lyric poet
must speedily set up a dialogue with the reader and adopt a
rhetorical posture in his very first line which can fill the silence that
has preceded it with a plausible replay of unspoken words. The rhetorical question is thus used by Elizabeth Barrett Browning:

> How do I love thee? Let me count the ways . . .

At once, imagination's ear supplies the unwritten lines that went
before: a pleading lover begging for reassurance of his lady's
commitment. Elizabeth's junior by 40 years, Friedrich Nietzsche,
introduces a tiny lyric of only six lines with questions that more
dramatically call up the interlocutor's unspoken prologue:

> Nicht mehr zurück? Und nicht hinan?
> Auch für die Gemse keine Bahn?

> (No escape from here, *you say* – not even for the light-footed antelope?)

It is worth considering what the question device does for both Nietzsche and Mrs Browning. It provides a dramatic index to a fictitious context, we have suggested, but, more important, it defines the *scope* of the poet's immediate concern. Mrs Browning will restrict herself to answering the question that opened her poem, Nietzsche to solving the intractable problem that his staccato questions show him to be facing.

Now, similar to the question in several interesting grammatical ways are constructions of negation and condition: for example in taking 'non-assertive' forms such as *any* (cf. Quirk *et al.* 1972, 4.127). The three are rhetorically alike also in providing a limitation of scope and a convenient means of fictively claiming common ground between writer and reader. When Donne begins his eighth Holy Sonnet with

> If faithful souls be alike glorified
> As angels

he is both prescribing his subject-matter and urging the reader to accept premises already established in discourse – however non-existent – between them. Or let us take Sonnet 116, Shakespeare's greatest, according to Douglas Bush:

> Let me not to the marriage of true minds
> Admit impediments; love is not love
> Which alters when it alteration finds
> Or bends with the remover to remove.
> O, no, it is an ever-fixèd mark
> That looks on tempests and is never shaken;
> It is the star to every wand'ring bark,
> Whose worth's unknown, although his height be taken.
> Love's not Time's fool, though rosy lips and cheeks
> Within his bending sickle's compass come;
> Love alters not with his brief hours and weeks,
> But bears it out even to the edge of doom.
>   If this be error, and upon me proved,
>   I never writ, nor no man ever loved.

Not merely do we again have the impression of plunging *in medias res*, with a form of words that brusquely obliges us ('Don't think that

I'm trying to knock fidelity . . .') to supply the essentials of
unwritten argument that precedes it: we also have a grammatical
form which – through negation – plainly prescribes the scope of the
argument that is to follow. There is then a second rhetorical negative, again predicting and prescribing what is to come: Love is not
love at all if it is fickle in the face of fickleness: *rather*, love is
essentially constant, something we can depend on as the sailor
depends on the stars by which he navigates.

There is a well-known rule that operates in very many languages,
including English, such that in the neutral or 'unmarked' uttering of a
clause we assign maximum prosodic prominence to the accented
syllable of the last semantically significant word. The whole phrase
in which this prominent syllable occurs will then be perceived as the
focus of the clause (cf. Quirk *et al.* 1972, 14.2f). Compare the
following sentences:

(8) Mary reviewed a book of his quite recently
(9) Quite recently Mary reviewed a book of his

Uttered normally (or read silently), (8) will have prosodic
prominence on the syllable /ri/ and the focus of the whole sentence
will be perceived as the temporal adjunct, *quite recently*, in which
this syllable lexically and grammatically functions. Example (9) has
the same meaning of truth-value (thus you cannot say both (8) and
(9) without tautology, and you cannot agree with one and deny the
other without contradiction), but the prosodic prominence falls on
book and thus the focus is the phrase in which *book* operates – the
noun phrase object, *a book of his*.

Let us now look at the beginning of these sentences. In (8), *Mary* is
wholly 'topicalized': that is, the form of the sentence presupposes
that Mary is the background for what is to be said (as perhaps
established in a previous sentence). In (9), while *Mary* remains the
grammatical subject, it is now the temporal phrase, *quite recently*,
that constitutes the 'topic', or common ground on which the sentence
grows. *Mary* is not of course wholly 'detopicalized'; this element
remains much more obviously part of the common ground between
the discourse participants than the phrase that is focused, *a book of
his*, with its tell-tale sign of 'newness', the indefinite article. But
although the subjects of sentences are normally in the area of 'topic'
(this after all is why the tradition has given us the name 'subject' for
this grammatical function), there is no reason why we should not

want to give the subject rhetorical focus and utter a sentence with a 'marked' and *non*-neutral form:

(10) /Màry reviewed a book of his#

In speech, we have intonation, pitch, stress, tempo to help us assign focus anywhere we want it. But in writing we have to program the reader without such assistance (italics are a poor substitute), and thus we seek lexical or grammatical alternatives that will move the item we want to focus into final position and thus ensure the reader's immediate reception of our intention:

John bought the car from Bill
Bill sold the car to John
John is in front of Mary
Mary is behind John

And if we want a written version of (10), that is, with the focus on *Mary*, ways of doing it so that a reader will assign focus correctly lie to hand in the passive and the 'cleft sentence' device:

(11) A book of his was reviewed by Mary
(12) It was Mary that reviewed a book of his

In (12), of course, there is a double focus: one on *Mary*, predictably, since this comes at the end of the preliminary clause; and another on *a book of his* at the end of the second clause. To get focus on a transitive verb phrase is not always easy in writing, but the cleft structure can be used to give a preliminary focus to the object, thus leaving the verb phrase in final position and hence carrying the second focus:

(13) It was a book of his that Mary reviewed

Alternatively, provided the agent (or active subject) is clear or irrelevant, we can again use the passive and, by deleting the agent, as in

(14) A book of his was reviewed

we achieve prosodic prominence on /vjud/, and hence the verb phrase *was reviewed* becomes the focus. A further, less common device is to wrench the object into initial position without the cleft structure, leaving the verb phrase in final focus position, as in

(15) A book of his Mary reviewed

We may now re-engage with the notion of scope and the function of interrogative and negative structures in defining it:

(16) What Mary reviewed was a book of his

This of course is really neither interrogative nor negative: it pretends to echo a previous question and uses the question-like device to indicate from the outset that the scope of Mary's reviewing is limited to a specific object to be revealed at the point of sentence focus. Nor is (17) really a negation, but the limiter adverb *only* is used to deny possible reviewings that Mary might have perfomed:

(17) Mary only reviewed a book of his

This is made explicit in the device (quite an extraordinary one when we reflect on it) found in the following:

(18) Mary never reviewed a book of his except (*or* until) quite recently
(19) Mary didn't review anything but a book of his
(20) Mary didn't do anything but review a book of his

The first part in each case is a plain lie in view of the exception that is made in the second, and the radical nature of the scoping device isolates and emphasizes the section that is focused. In (18) and (19), scope and focus coincide in the time adjunct and the noun phrase object respectively, but in (20), while the focus is again the noun phrase object, the scope extends to the whole 'predication', an abstraction broadly covering the 'lexical verb' and any part of the predicate following it (see Quirk *et al.* 1972, 2.2, and the further references provided there). It is the fact that the negative particle regularly precedes this section ('Mary did not *review the book*') that makes it natural for *only* to occupy the same position, indicating the scope limitation well in advance of the point that is actually focused. Thus (17) and the following would normally be interpreted as identical:

Mary reviewed only a book of his

That is to say, it is relatively rare to find *only* directing the focus on to a following verb, as in

Mary only reviewed (she didn't publish or rewrite or . . .) a book of his.

Indeed, it is often difficult to conceive of a verb carrying alone a contrastive focus in this way. Thus in

(21) Mary only comes to see me occasionally

only will be taken to indicate scope limitation throughout the predication but also to direct (emphasized) focus to the normally expected point, the concluding clausal element: thus *(only . . .) occasionally*.

Let us now consider the situation in which we wish to include a long and complex noun phrase in our scope but with emphatic (contrastive) focus on only part of it. For example:

(22) Mary only reviewed books of his that she genuinely admired

The limitation to the subset of his books may be pinpointed more sharply by the use of the demonstrative to correlate with the relative clause:

(23) Mary only reviewed *those* books of his *that* she genuinely admired

Combining this structure with the object-fronting earlier illustrated in (15), we have a rather formidable structure, typically involving discontinuity of the noun phrase (Quirk *et al.* 1972, 13.74, 14.41).

(24) *Those books of his* Mary reviewed *that she genuinely admired*

We may now turn to a short poem ('Ghosts') by Elizabeth Jennings, which begins with a sentence of just this form:

> Those houses haunt in which we leave
> Something undone. It is not those
> 3 Great words or silences of love
>
> That spread their echoes through a place
> And fill the locked-up unbreathed gloom.
> 6 Ghosts do not haunt with any face
>
> That we have known; they only come
> With arrogance to thrust at us
> 9 Our own omissions in a room.
>
> The words we would not speak they use,
> The deeds we dared not act they flaunt,
> 12 Our nervous silences they bruise;
>
> It is our helplessness they choose
> And our refusals that they haunt.

The striking opening by means of which the poet 'thrusteth into the middest' clearly entails a fairly precise understanding by the reader of the unspoken argument that has preceded this 'beginning'. Indeed, we cannot read the poem without rapidly reconstructing this argument as a precondition to accepting as rational the grammar and rhetoric of what follows. That is, we allow ourselves to be put in the position of one who has just stated the generally received view of ghosts and their reasons for haunting: 'Well, we all know that hauntings take place in houses where something extraordinary has been done.' The poem then proceeds to reject this view: 'No, no – those houses . . . in which we leave something undone.' The discontinuous noun phrase structure, as in example (24) above, ensures that there is an early and very precise scoping, and at the same time it equally ensures that the normal place of prosodic prominence will sharply focus the point of greatest contrast with the normal view of haunting: *undone*. The affixal negation achieves something more. Compare

> The meal was not eaten
> The meal was uneaten

Whereas the former is uncommitted as to the speaker's judgment, the latter gives a somewhat slanted point of view: the speaker implies that he thought it would (or *should*) have been eaten. Now, in contrast to the general view that hauntings take place because something extraordinary (a) *has* been done, and (b) should *not* have been done, Elizabeth Jennings is claiming the double converse: something has *not* been done that *should* have been done; the haunting is because we have left 'something *undone*.'[1]

The remainder of the poem is a detailed and evocative expansion of this point.

Lines 2–5 use the cleft sentence construction to give preliminary focus on the subject ('those . . . words . . . of love'), as in example

---

[1] There is a second use of *un*-negation with similar effect in *unbreathed gloom*, line 5: in a properly ordered world, we do not expect rooms to be locked up and the air to be 'unbreathed.' While noting that *un*- with past participles occurs in sequences like *an uneaten meal* 'but not, as a rule, *an eaten meal*', Zimmer (1964, 36) misses the significant point that this type of negation involves the additional connotative factor that we might paraphrase as 'counter to expectation'. See further, Stein 1978, Ch. 3. Shelley's 'To a Skylark' has a number of interesting examples in the opening stanzas: the bird is like an *unbodied joy*, singing *unseen* and *unbidden* with *unpremeditated art*.

(12) above, with early scoping by *not*. It is worth noting what is lost if we attempt a less rhetorically oriented syntagmatic organization: 'Those great words do not spread their echoes'; this form of the sentence is totally unpoised for the essential point: '*rather*, something else does this.'

Lines 6–7 contain a sentence with prosodic prominence on *known*, thus focusing the instrumental phrase *with . . . face . . . known*, but – through negative scoping – forcing a contrast on the postmodification. It is not that ghosts haunt facelessly (still less, of course, that 'Ghosts do not haunt'): they haunt with faces that are unknown, in the sense that what has not happened has no 'face' and it is precisely the non-event that we find haunting. The syntactic device resembles that in examples (18) to (20) above, and its rhetorical drive is completed in lines 7–9, 'not *that* but *this*', scoping with *only* as in (17) and (21), and placing in focus the noun phrase object *our own omissions in a room*, which through the rhyme scheme is prosodically linked (and suggestively equated) with *the . . . unbreathed gloom* of line 5.

The stanza of lines 10–12 consists of sentences having the form of example (15), with the three verbs in focus through the fronting of the three objects, but with a preliminary focus on the object phrases themselves by reason of their dislocation. This strategy of double focus is repeated in the two closing lines, which have the less striking, more prosaic form of cleft sentence to front the objects, as in (13). The result is not merely a very effective terminal focus on what has naturally been the key verb in the poem, *haunt*, but a rhyme link with *flaunt* (line 11), which neatly summarizes the essential activity of ghosts which the poem has urged.

An ending that we have known, we sense, from the beginning.

References

Kermode, Frank 1966: *The Sense of an Ending*. New York: Oxford University Press.

Li, C.N. 1976: *Subject and Topic*. New York: Academic Press.

Quirk, R., Greenbaum, S., Leech, G. and Svartvik, J. 1972: *A Grammar of Contemporary English*. London and New York: Longman.

Stein, G. 1978: *Studies in the Function of the Passive*. Tübingen: Narr.

Zimmer, K. E. 1964: *Affixal Negation in English and Other Languages*. Supplement to *Word* 20.

Index